Light Shines Through the Broken Pieces

A Father and Son's Journey to Healing

Matthew Fisher
Steven Fisher

(c) 2022 Matthew Fisher and Steven Fisher
All Rights Reserved.

No part of this publication may be reproduced, stored in a retrieval system, or transmitted, in any form or by any means, electronic, mechanical, photocopying, recording, or otherwise, without the written permission of the authors.

First published by On the Write Path Publishing
5023 W. 120th Ave. #228
Broomfield, CO 80020
martinmcleanlit@aol.com

On The Write Path
PUBLISHING

Paperback ISBN:979-8-88590-212-0
eBook ISBN: 979-8-88590-213-7

This book is printed on acid-free paper.
Printed in the United States of America

Learn more about Matthew and Steven, and gain access to content on self-development and relationship skills on their website.

Fishertransformation.com

The names and identifying details of certain individuals have been changed to protect their privacy.

This book is dedicated to anyone struggling with mental health and substance abuse problems or loves someone who is.

We would also like to thank Matthew's mother and Steven's loving wife, Liz, for her constant love, patience and understanding through the years and as we went through the process of writing this book. A special acknowledgment to Matthew's brothers and Steven's sons, Craig and Connor. Their wisdom and intelligence is greatly admired and loved. Many thanks to Trish for showing up when we needed her the most, and a special thanks to Mile Hi Church for always being a place where anything is possible. Love and blessings to Jess, Suzanne, Art and all the other dear friends who supported us through this time in our lives.

CONTENTS

Introduction xi

Chapter 1: Embracing Vulnerability 13
    Lesson: Sometimes the strongest and most courageous thing we can do is be willing to admit we are vulnerable and need help. . 17

Chapter 2: Only Love Is Real 20
    Lesson: Releasing fears and judgments lets us realize the only thing that ever is and ever will be real is love. 22

Chapter 3: Heartache, Trauma and Forgiveness 25
    Lesson: Accepting the past lets us take control of where our lives go from here. 29

Chapter 4: The Masks We Wear 31
    Lesson: Breaking out of the mask. 34

Chapter 5: Anger Management 37
    Lesson: True conflict resolution requires us to let go of "being right." 39

Chapter 6: The Fight **42**
    Lesson: Setting healthy interpersonal boundaries. 45

Chapter 7: Broken Masculinity **48**
    Lesson: A more mature definition of manhood. 49

Chapter 8: Codependency and Relationships **51**
    Lesson: Seeing people for who they really are. 56
    Lesson: Love is letting go. 57

Chapter 9: Wherever We Go, There We Are **60**
    Lesson: Happiness comes from within. 61

Chapter 10: Finding Passions and Facing Fears **63**
    Lesson: Creating change from a place of love and passion. 65

Chapter 11: Lessons in the Hot Springs **68**
    Lesson: Taking time for self-care. 69

Chapter 12: Sharing Our Burdens Together **71**
    Lesson: Listening without expectation or judgment. 75
    Lesson: Learning to share our burdens together. 76

Chapter 13: The Light Shines in the Darkness **78**
    Lesson: Finding hope and faith in life's hardest moments. 79

Chapter 14: Wilderness Therapy ... 81
Lesson: Working through trauma and processing experiences. 83

Chapter 15: On the Turning Away ... 87
Lesson: Building personal and community resilience. ... 88

Lesson: Finding our way past excessive individualism. ... 90

Chapter 16: Calm Within the Storm ... 94
Lesson: Letting go of compulsive thinking and action. ... 96

Lesson: Mirror neurons and empathy. ... 98

Chapter 17: Radical Self-Responsibility ... 100
Lesson: Release blame and take responsibility for our reality. 102

Chapter 18: My Best Friend ... 104
Lesson: Embracing unconditional love. ... 105

Chapter 19: The Gift of Pain ... 107
Lesson: Finding healing and connection by embracing our emotions and pain. ... 109

Chapter 20: A Father's Love ... 112
Lesson: Love shown by consistent, positive attention is vital for a child's healthy development. ... 115

Lesson: Happiness comes from changing our perspective ... 119

Chapter 21: Healing Your Family Tree 122
    Lesson: Understanding the big picture of our family patterns frees us from repeating them. 124

Chapter 22: My Mother's Love 127
    Lesson: Holding our center in the midst of conflict. 129

Chapter 23: We Are All Just Angry Kittens 131
    Lesson: There is no "them" or "other." We are all on the same team. 134

Chapter 24: Love Is Not Weak 137
    Lesson: Learning to see love as a strength. 138

Conclusion 141

INTRODUCTION

MATTHEW

Becoming healed, whole adults requires us to embrace the parts of ourselves we are afraid and ashamed of, and it takes acknowledging what has shaped us. It means taking responsibility for where we go from here and letting go of hopelessness, self-pity, shame and despair. My journey has not been the easiest nor the hardest, but it has made me into who I am. Finding peace with myself paves the way to shine brighter in the world and brings out my gifts and talents to be of service to others.

What I have learned on this journey is that no matter how many times we get knocked down, what counts is how fast we decide to get up. I have faced drug abuse, depression, thoughts of suicide, feeling lost and hopeless in myself, and have seen many of my friends, clients, and community face these same problems. There was a time when it seemed a long shot to me that I could come out as a healthy adult, but through the help of many amazing mentors, friends and family, here I am. Currently, I am pursuing a degree in addiction counseling and I work at a drug and alcohol treatment center.

Activists, teachers, kids, leaders, really all of us, are becoming burnt out. Helplessness and despair have reached societal-wide proportions. Our society today is faced with a tremendous amount of addiction and mental health problems. We are faced with unprecedented challenges in climate change, a toxic political environment, gun violence and teen suicide, just to name a few. We are strained to the edges as parents, mental health workers, teachers and friends, trying to prepare the next generation for these challenges, while coping with them ourselves. The world we are living in is changing, and the decisions we make now and the values we instill in our children, students, and peers will have impacts lasting for generations.

In light of this, it is essential for people to reconnect with each other and the world to find a new sense of empowerment and meaning. I have found that change doesn't come from guilt or anger, but rather from finding something larger than ourselves, and letting the wonder of it lead us to places we never thought possible. In this book, I will share stories from my own life and the lives of others that have impacted me. I hope my personal experiences and others' stories will help anyone going through similar problems, and provide understanding, helpful ideas for those who love and raise struggling children.

CHAPTER 1
EMBRACING VULNERABILITY

MATTHEW

A lot of my life I felt angry, out of control, scared and alone. The brighter aspects of my personality such as my curiosity, compassion, and love for my family, were buried under manic outbursts, drug abuse, and a mind-numbing depression. I felt lost and alone. I experienced myself as disconnected from my family, my community, and myself. In my own bubble of self-hatred and fear, it was hard to see how it was possible to reach out to others, make friends, or be a part of a community. Though I lost sight of the light and goodness in myself, my parents and a lot of amazing people around me never did.

A huge turning point happened for me one night when I took some LSD and painkillers at a friend's house, and I came very close to losing my mind. The room around me started to spin and I felt a heavy anxiety rise up in my stomach. I told my friend I was starting to freak out, and she said I was going to ruin her trip and I should leave. My panic increased to the point where I couldn't talk. "At least give me your keys before you go so you don't drive," she said. I numbly handed her the keys and walked out the door. It was midnight in March and about 20 degrees outside. I was so high that I forgot my shoes and jacket. I wandered around the neighborhood for a while and got lost. Every house looked the same. I eventually found my way back to my car, which thankfully was unlocked. I sat shoeless, in a short-sleeved shirt in my car with no heat, slowly losing the battle with my own inner demons.

All of the fear, doubt, and self-hatred I had been living with was thrown in my face. I remember going through my phone and even trying to call some of my "friends" who told me they couldn't deal with more bullshit right now. I realized how alone I was and how much I had pushed away those around me.

In a moment of clarity, I concluded that I needed help. I made a call to my parents, not an easy decision as we had fought over my drug use since I was 13. They managed to find me, despite the fact I couldn't remember my friend's address and gave very incoherent directions. Seeing my mom knock on my car door was one of the most incredible and relieving moments of my life. Riding back, I kept repeating, "I lost all the love, where did it go? I lost it," and my father told me over and over again, "It never left, Matt, it never left. It's right here."

I went in and out of some form of psychosis for about a month. I couldn't even walk around the block without panicking let alone work, and thankfully my parents were willing to support me. My sanity eventually returned and from then on, I was determined to get my shit together. I started going to therapy again, I enrolled in college, and I started taking care of my body, mind and soul. The next few years were some of the best of my life, and I found amazing friends, adventures, and a sense of purpose. I found a passion for outdoor education and mental health, and my friends and family supported me in my mental health and sobriety.

STEVEN

We found Matt sitting alone, shivering in the driver's seat of our blue Hyundai Santa Fe in the parking lot of some random apartment complex across town. A thin sheet of white snow covered the parking lot and whitened the roofs of the apartment buildings all around us, in the silence of the night. It was about 1:00 a.m. on a Saturday, and Matt only had on his faded jeans and a flimsy short sleeved t-shirt, in his bare feet. The car was dark and silent with no heat, and my son was shivering uncontrollably. When we knocked on his window, he turned his head and I saw intense fear as well as tears of relief in his eyes.

Matt had woken us up from a deep sleep when he called about 45 minutes earlier. It was shortly after midnight, and he said that he was in the middle of a really bad acid trip. He told us he was lost and didn't know how to get home. Liz and I were dressed and out the door in about five minutes, and I was driving in the general direction of Aurora, Colorado. Liz stayed on the phone with Matt while he was doing his best to give directions to his location. I would call out the landmarks along the way, and Liz would relay Matt's confused and uncertain directions. By some miracle, when we pulled up in the parking lot of the apartment complex, hoping we were at the right place, there was our blue Hyundai Santa Fe. Matt sitting alone, shivering in the driver's seat, looked so small, afraid and pitiful. It just broke my heart.

He was so incredibly relieved to see us, but that relief only lasted for a few seconds as he started to sob uncontrollably while Liz and I silently hugged him tightly. He told us he had got in an argument with the girl he was seeing and some friends in her apartment while they were tripping together. He said he could not go back because the negativity was too much for him. We didn't know which apartment it was, so we just got him in the car with me, and Liz drove behind us in the Hyundai all the way home. Matt was crying, anxious and depressed, and he kept repeating, "I lost all the love, where did it go? I lost it." I told him that I loved him and his mom loved him, and the love was right here and it never left. I was so scared for my son, and experienced such a deep and profound love for him on that ride home. I felt so powerless to help him, and I remembered that little boy he had been with bright eyes, a cheerful smile, and endless questions about life. I prayed he would find that joy in his life again.

When we got home, we settled him in bed. He was still tripping hard and we were with him, talking to him as he slowly calmed down. We tried to stay awake, but were exhausted. Sometime later, Liz shook me awake. She had been half asleep, like a mother with one ear out for her infant in the middle of the night, and realized we had drifted off to sleep and Matt was gone. We panicked. We looked for him all over the house and backyard, and he was nowhere to be found. After a frantic search, we finally found him about ten minutes later, meditating under a tree in a park across the street. We got him back home, and the rest of the night his psychedelic experience was fairly uneventful as he started to come down by morning.

Over the next month, the darkness of intense anxiety and depression stayed with Matt. Liz and I hovered over him like mother hens as we nursed him back to life. He got back into counseling, and started to get serious about his self-care with diet, exercise, and lots of sleep. He became invested in healthy living and decided to go back to college.

Matt had struggled with anxiety, drugs, alcohol and depression through his teen years, and always had a hard time finding friends and a group where he belonged. After that night, he never went back to that girl or those friends, and he started to reach out to individuals that supported his recovery. The next few months, I watched him slowly emerge from the darkness that had clouded his life for so long. Over time, the fear for my precious son faded as he began to turn a corner in his life. He began reading every book he could find on healing and recovery, and I would see titles like *Healing Depression* lying around the house for years after that.

Rock bottom looks different for everyone, and this was one of those times for Matt. While it was a painful and difficult experience, I am grateful for the deep wisdom and compassion for others that he has developed by working through these experiences and facing his trauma. I am moved by the strength of his character and love for others, and his commitment to making a difference in the world.

Lesson: Sometimes the strongest and most courageous thing we can do is be willing to admit we are vulnerable and need help.

A few years after this experience, I was having a conversation with a friend. He had worked through his own struggles with addiction and had helped me and many other people through a lot. He told me that he was able to help others because he had stood in their shoes. He understood what it was like to be in their struggle, yet also knew what it was like to make it to the other side. In mythology, someone would come across the path of a shaman or healer because they themselves needed healing. Having walked through pain and struggle, the wounded healer had the ability to empathize with others, yet having come out the other side, they were able to provide perspective and healing.

In my generation, there is an unprecedented amount of suicide, violence, depression, anxiety, addiction and countless other signs that show people are suffering. I have had my own battles, but I've heard countless stories from friends, girlfriends, clients and people I barely know, about how much conflict and pain they are going through. I have also seen incredible strength, compassion, awareness, and a deep desire for change from these same people.

Struggle and hardship have valuable lessons to teach us if we are willing to listen. They tell us to value and be grateful for those we love, to care more about the people and environment around us, and to be gentler and kinder in the face of hate. We have the choice to allow these experiences to be a catalyst for growth and change, but we have to be willing to face, heal and learn from them. A lot of the time, our first reaction is to numb ourselves so we don't have to feel anything so horrible ever again. Yet, when we numb out the bad, we deaden the good as well. When we can't feel fear or sadness, we can't feel love and joy. When we have the courage to face the darkness, we find incredible light. And right now, the world and the people in our lives need this light more than ever.

For me, vulnerability was the major lesson of that night. Vulnerability means sharing any part of ourselves that might be afraid of feeling hurt or criticized. We avoid sharing our feelings, ideas, struggles, and weaknesses because we are afraid of being judged or hurt. What is the impact of this? We are afraid to ask for help, we avoid sharing our aspirations, dreams and big ideas, and we hide the parts of ourselves that have the most to offer. In this culture a lot of us, especially men, are conditioned out of vulnerability.

Throughout the disappointments, mistakes, and hurt we all go through in life, it's very easy to shut down parts of ourselves and create an armor that protects us from being vulnerable. But in doing so, we shut down our ability to connect and grow. Vulnerability is essential for us to heal and achieve our highest form of self-expression.

Opening up to someone, taking accountability for our actions, and admitting that change is necessary, can be extremely hard, but it is necessary to have a fulfilling life and relationships. This does not mean we should go around telling our deepest darkest secrets to everyone, and blasting them on social media. Part of cultivating vulnerability is learning who to trust. If we share something with a person who does not respect our privacy or boundaries, and breaks our trust, it will cause us to retreat further away from expressing vulnerability.

Questions:

1. What are parts of yourself (ideas, passions, fears, weaknesses) that you hide from others?

2. Do you avoid asking for help or support? If so, in what ways?

3. What are some ways you could express yourself more authentically?

4. What are some ways you could lean on others more for support?

CHAPTER 2
ONLY LOVE IS REAL

STEVEN

Some years ago, Matthew came to me and asked me to write "I love you" on a piece of paper. I saw already written on that paper were a few other lines of the same phrase, "I love you," and I asked him what that was all about. He told me he had requested his brothers and mother all write that phrase, and he was going to engrave it permanently on his arm as a tattoo. He's never going to regret getting that tattoo.

Matthew has worked really hard to overcome his problems and become a remarkable, strong and loving human being. He has a degree in outdoor education, and he's working on a degree in psychology. Matthew is a yoga instructor, he's been a wilderness therapy guide, he's led wilderness trips, and he currently works helping men at an alcohol and drug rehab facility. My relationship with Matt has been really difficult at times over the years. Last week, he told me, "I know there is this wall between us. I know I was really hard to raise, but I love you and I'm so grateful to have you in my life."

I responded, "Matt, you're right and I'm so sorry." Over the 25 years of his life, this has been a painful subject for him and me because it's true. I have always felt more emotionally comfortable with his younger twin brothers who are both amazing people themselves. Through childhood and their teenage years, Matthew's brothers, Craig and Connor, never challenged me or called me out so hard like Matthew did, and they never rebelled quite so aggressively to my face. As a teen, he would tell me that I liked them better than I liked him. This time, he just said that I have an emotional wall with him that I don't have with them, and I noticed the growth in his perceptions of the subtleties of this often painful dynamic in our family. Today he does know how much I love him and I believe he knows that I can't imagine loving him or his brothers any more or less than each other.

All Matthew said in response was, "I forgive you, Dad. I forgive you." What I also noticed was that when Matthew said this to me last week, there was no anger or hurt, only love for his father. He tells me every day how much he loves me, and how grateful he is that I am his dad, and I know he means it. One of Matthew's many gifts is that he is a straight talker and he never says anything he doesn't mean, but now he's learned how to be that direct with kindness in a truly non-judgmental way. I felt the tears welling up as he called me out last week, and his loving strength, clarity and honesty are deeply impressive and moving to me.

This emotional wound between us is a family legacy passed down from my relationship with my father as well, because my dad consistently said to me over the years, "Steve, out of all my seven children, you gave me the most trouble." This was because, like Matthew, I also had trouble with speaking out directly and honestly when I probably should have kept my mouth shut. Whenever I had a problem with something Dad said or did, I would call him out and challenge him more directly than my siblings would. That was probably uncomfortable for him like it was for me with Matthew. Karma is a bitch sometimes, and I am profoundly grateful for Matthew helping me heal my family legacy of broken relationships between fathers and sons by learning to communicate honestly and directly with kindness and without any blame and criticism.

Matthew knows that despite all our painful struggles and our ups and downs over the years, the truth between us is that we love each other, and nothing else matters. He knows that only love is real and everything else is just an illusion made of smoke and mirrors. Even though as a child I often didn't like some things my father did, or I struggled with how he didn't have time for me because he worked so much, I realize now that everything my father did was because of his love for me and mom and all my siblings. The truth of my father and my son is love, and nothing else really matters.

Lesson: Releasing fears and judgments lets us realize the only thing that ever is and ever will be real is love.

Once people sort through the layers of fear and ego baggage that they have, they always find this same love at the heart of themselves and every other human being. Learning how to recognize this love and act from this loving place is what Matthew did for me in our conversation and it is life transforming. This is also what I teach as a therapist, and I have seen this transformation occur hundreds of times when people begin to sort through their own layers of fear and ego baggage to see the core truth of love within themselves and in their family, lovers and friends.

Every day as a therapist I have the remarkable opportunity to be with people to process the depths of their life issues and open to a greater experience of love for themselves and for their loved ones in a deeper and greater way. People often ask me, "How can you do this all day long with everyone pouring out their suffering and pain in your office?" My answer is that it is so easy, because what I am primarily present to is the greatness of this human being in front of me. I am so present to the depth of love they feel for their family and loved ones. Whatever they are going through, all they want and all they ever wanted is to love and be loved. They just got confused a bit on how to find that love.

The more I work with people and regardless of the issues they bring into my office, I am more and more aware of the profound truth that who we are as human beings is love, plain and simple. This profound truth is just too simple for complicated minds. We tend to see the problems and dysfunction in ourselves and others and the world, and we lose sight of the simple truth of love that is our nature. However, when we look beyond the labels we put on ourselves, others and the world, all we find is people who want to love and be loved. While people may often be misguided on how to find that love, it doesn't change their nature.

Despite appearances, there is nothing but love. Everything else is all smoke and mirrors. This doesn't mean to ignore the problems of the world, or be blind to our difficulties and struggles in life. It is important to be practical and realistic about whatever problems we face, but it's even more important to ground our awareness on the fundamental reality of love that is the foundation of our connection with all life. Regardless of appearances, we are all simply different aspects of the One, experiencing itself from different points of view. Our lives are an expression of this love whenever we choose to see it, live it and know it.

Questions:

1. Who are the people in your life that you love and make life meaningful? Write a list of all of these people.

2. How do you express your love to them? If you struggle expressing your feelings, what blocks the expression?

3. What are some ways you could be freer in expressing your love for others? I invite you to take action on this!

CHAPTER 3

HEARTACHE, TRAUMA AND FORGIVENESS

MATTHEW

As a teen, I had very intense mood swings. I was diagnosed with a mood disorder. I was either incredibly depressed, or angry and manic. These extremes tore apart my relationships with my friends and family, and made me lose sight of who I was for a long time.

Growing up, I was a really happy kid. My childhood was wonderful and full of excitement, joy and love. We lived very close to my grandparents and my mom's siblings and their families, and I was constantly surrounded with caring and supportive people. We would all go over to my grandmother's house for holidays and family gatherings. My grandmother was the life of the party, and made everyone around her feel loved and welcome. Both my parents had master's degrees in counseling. My dad worked as a therapist, and Mom did therapy for a little while, but became a Montessori teacher when I was born. My two twin brothers were born almost two years after me. We were all pretty close and played together all of the time.

When I was about six years old, my mom got a job in Colorado and my parents decided to move the family there. I was really angry about moving, and missed all of my friends and family in Mississippi. I remember driving up to our new house in Golden, Colorado, and seeing snow for the first time. It was really exciting, and made me feel a lot better about the move. The first year we were in Colorado, there was a massive ten-year snow storm and everything in our neighborhood was covered in over five feet of snow for weeks. I remember building a snowman over ten feet tall!

I started class at a Montessori school. In kindergarten, I had a lot of friends and every day was an adventure. I changed classes in first grade, and went to the school's other location. Around 3rd grade, my mood swings got a lot more intense. I was violent toward my brothers, regularly beating them up and picking on them. I was incredibly lonely and depressed.

One afternoon when I was in the 4th grade, my parents were opening a new office for my dad's counseling practice. During this event, a friend used to come over to hang out with my brothers and me. I was becoming a lot angrier and more antisocial that year, and understandably, my friend decided that spending time with my brothers was a lot more enjoyable. My brothers and my friend were avoiding me, playing in the parking lot of the office. I walked over to one of my brothers, pulled him off his bike, and started kicking him. Someone tugged me off of him, and I ran home. My parents stormed in the house, and at first, they were furious and yelling at me. I started crying, saying I couldn't help it. At that time in my life, when I had an outburst, I felt out of control and overwhelmed by fear and anger.

After beating up my brother, I was never quite as violent. I still had outbursts, but I knew I had crossed a line. The summer of 7th grade I started smoking and drinking, and a friend's older brother introduced me to marijuana. I found that it helped me numb the pain and control my emotions.

STEVEN

It was the day of the grand opening of my counseling office which was down the street from our house. There was a lot to do, and our boys who were in elementary and middle school were playing with a friend in the parking lot. I was greeting people and showing them our new offices, and sharing information about my counseling services. All of our friends and acquaintances and people I didn't know were stopping by to see our new space.

Just then, my wife's boss came in and informed me that our oldest son, Matthew, had beaten up one of our twins in the parking lot. Liz and I rushed out and saw him crying and Matthew standing off to the side, angry and silent. I remember rushing over to pick up my son who was sobbing uncontrollably. After a few minutes, Liz took him home while I went back and canceled the rest of the open house.

At that point, I heard that my wife's boss had seen our son on the ground in the parking lot, crying while Matthew was kicking him repeatedly, and she had gone over to stop the beat down. This was one of the lowest points of my life. I was feeling concerned and scared for our son, while also feeling an overwhelming mix of emotions toward Matthew, and guilty for our family conflicts that had led us to this point. Obviously, I was also embarrassed to have our family trauma displayed for the public at the grand opening of my counseling office. The irony of the situation was overwhelming, but I was more concerned for the well-being of my children in that moment.

When I got home a short time later, Liz was holding our son who was still crying and distraught. We sat for a while comforting him, and I began trying to understand what happened. As it turned out, Matthew and his twin brothers were playing with a mutual friend and Matthew had gotten upset because the friend wanted to play with his brothers, but didn't want to hang out with Matthew. Our twins and this friend had begun avoiding Matthew, and his feelings of being left out and shunned by his brothers and his good friend had gotten the best of him. That's when he beat up his brother in the parking lot.

This pattern of conflict with Matthew feeling inadequate, isolated and left out, and our twins feeling scared of their big brother's anger, had been playing out for years. This sibling abuse from Matthew toward our twins had gotten worse when they were very young and we moved to Colorado. As parents, Liz and I had struggled with this issue for years. The twins were more socially gifted and everyone loved them, while Matthew struggled to make friends and constantly felt left out, alone, and jealous of his brothers for getting all the positive attention.

This issue started when the twins were born. Matthew had been an only child up to that point, and he felt knocked off the throne big time when his younger brothers came along. He was clear in letting me know that he was upset because the twins stole all the attention. When they were only a few months old, Matthew told me, "I want to throw them in the trash!"

Liz and I had struggled with this conflict between our boys for years and honestly, we were not as firm with Matthew as we needed to be because we felt his pain. We didn't want to take sides or have him feel rejected or left out. This pattern of conflict had also probably been the source of the greatest trauma for the twins as well.

Over the years, Liz and I have gone back to them and apologized many times for not protecting them enough.

Lesson: Accepting the past lets us take control of where our lives go from here.

While not all of my memories of where I grew up were happy, I will always be connected to my past there. I'll never forget the trails my parents took me hiking, the street where I learned to skateboard, the gas station where my brothers and I spent all our allowance on candy, the elementary school where I made some of my first friends, and when I learned how to become a master negotiator at the lunch table (my mom never packed good lunches).

The middle school I hated, the high school where I met my first girlfriend, the slide where I kissed a girl for the first time, the park where my friends left me, passed out after getting drunk for the first time, the woods; I needed to forget about everything for a bit. All of these places hold memories, good and bad, and I will always keep them close to my heart.

Whether or not they cause my heart to ache or leap for joy, they are a part of me and I will always hold onto them. A lot of my past was really hard, but it helped me become stronger, wiser, and more compassionate. While I wouldn't wish it on anyone else, I am happy with who I am now. The depth of love and joy I have in all of my relationships from having to work through my inner demons, made it worth it.

While I still struggle with getting over trauma, depression and anxiety, and a lot of the time my past seems to be driving the bus, I believe that we are always able to overcome our past and become someone new. We can let go of our anger and forgive, and let our sorrow soften us and make us kinder rather than cripple us. We can take a deep breath and overcome our deepest fears.

Our early lives determine a lot about us. We aren't given any control over the parents we have, the places we grow up, or the people we went to school with. To me, this is not a cop out. This is accepting the cards we've been dealt and moving on from there. While the person we are now may have been created by external circumstances, we always have a choice in who we choose to be in the present moment, and the person we become in the future. We also embrace that not everything in our lives is in our control, and acknowledge that we need help from others to learn and grow.

Questions:

1. In what ways does your past define you? How are you continually replaying out the patterns of conflict or conflict avoidance based on the fears and emotional baggage from your past?

2. In what ways do you struggle to move on?

3. How can you begin to write a new story of your life?

CHAPTER 4
THE MASKS WE WEAR

MATTHEW

The first time I bought marijuana, I hastily smoked a little bit with a friend after "procuring it" from an older kid on the bus, and hid it in my room. I have never been able to hide anything from my mother. She has a certain sixth sense when it comes to things going on in our family. When I came home from school the next day, the bag of weed was sitting on our kitchen table. I immediately got angry at my parents and tried to blame them for going into my room. They told me to get into the car and drove me down to the police station.

Looking back, I understand that my drinking and drug use had made them scared for my safety, and they didn't know what else to do. However, at that moment, I thought they hated me. I remember the incredulous look on the police officer's face as my parents handed him a bag of weed. In some ways, it was good for me. I was forced to go to drug classes and get drug tested. However, I quickly started up again as soon as I was done with drug testing.

When I was in 8th grade, I was finally shown the spot where all of the "cool" high schoolers met up to smoke and drink in the woods. I didn't have a lot of friends in middle school, and this was in my mind an initiation into a better world of friends and partying. These kids turned out to not particularly care much about anything, except for getting drunk and high. Go figure. One day, I drank a lot of whiskey at a friend's house before coming over to the couch, and when I got there, I continued to drink and smoke. I was unable to talk coherently, and the other kids started making fun of me. One kid put out a cigarette on my arm. Eventually, it got dark and most of my "friends" left.

My dad had been looking for me all day, and finally found me passed out in the woods with a few stragglers who were still drinking. He told them he was going to call the cops. That week, I received several threats from the kids I had thought were my friends. One guy everyone called "dough boy" told everyone he would kick my ass the next time I saw them. He had apparently been in a gang at one point, but he was really just a 30 year old that worked at a pizza shop and sold cigarettes to high school kids. I told my dad about this situation, accused him of ruining my life, and said he was going to get me killed. He looked me dead in the face and said, "I'm not afraid of a bunch of deadbeat kids that are threatening my son. I am more than happy to call the police again."

I was still mad at my dad, but seeing his willingness to protect me helped me release my fear around those kids, and enabled me to let go of my desire to be accepted by them. Unfortunately, this did not stop me from trying to use drugs and alcohol to self-medicate and hide from what I was feeling. The more I turned to drugs and pornography to feel something, the less I felt anything, and that feeling of numbness and emotional disconnection continued to get worse. I remember at times looking at myself in the mirror and seeing a stranger. I was so focused on being who I thought people would like, or what would gain me acceptance, that I started losing the sense of who I truly was. I started smoking OxyContin with some friends and got really involved in the rave scene, doing a lot of ecstasy and whatever strange pills I came across.

STEVEN

When Matthew was about thirteen, he started hanging out with sketchy "friends" and using marijuana and alcohol more. Liz and I were concerned and tried to restrict his activities, but there was no stopping him. One day, I was out looking for Matt when I heard he was partying with some high school kids in the area. A teen downtown in our community directed me to a path into the woods behind a local church. Liz and I slowly walked down the path amid trees and foliage, and it started to curve up a slope heading up the mountain behind the church. About a hundred yards into the trees and undergrowth, at the end of the path, there was a small clearing where we found a couple of teens sitting on a couch. The moment felt surreal, like a scene from *Alice in Wonderland*. They didn't know Matthew's whereabouts, and they probably would not have told me if they did, but they were polite in a disassociated and stoned sort of way. Returning down the trail, we found Matt lying on the ground beside the path, passed out drunk. My heart was in my shoes, and I was fighting back tears as I gently picked him up and carried him to our house which was less than a mile away.

As angry and rebellious as he was at that time, he was my son, and all I saw was the hurt and emotional scars that were driving his anger and poor choices in life. We got back to the house and I softly put him on his bed to sleep it off. As I pulled the covers over him and I walked out of the room, I said a silent prayer for my son who was lost in his own pain and anguish.

A few days later, Matthew confronted me and said I had put him in danger because I had snitched about the location of their hideout to the police. I told Matt that I would be happy to call the police and deal with any deadbeat kids who were threatening my son, and that seemed to help Matt feel better.

Liz and I were racking our brains to think of any way to get through to him about the consequences of his choices. So, a short time later when Liz found some marijuana stashed in his room, we decided to turn Matt and his weed into the police. We talked to Matt, and drove him and the marijuana to the local police precinct. I still remember my feelings of deep sadness and the incredulous look of surprise on the police officer's face when we handed him the bag of weed, right in front of the precinct, and quietly asked him to charge Matt with possession. Matt's head was down, but he cooperated as he got booked and charged. Matt went to court and ultimately had to complete substance abuse classes with no further legal consequences, but he told me he had lost trust in me out of this situation.

I understood that his losing trust in me made perfect sense to his thirteen-year-old brain, but over time he would likely come around. This has proven to be true, and looking back, my relationship with Matthew has just become stronger out of these conflicts.

Lesson: Breaking out of the mask.

The mask is the way we present ourselves to the world, and is made of all the ideas we have about what people want to see from us, and how we want others to see us. We often create a narrative about ourselves based on our unresolved fears and self-esteem issues, worrying about things others may not even be thinking about us.

Even if others are upset with us, or if we allow our identity to be shaped at the whim of others, we will dampen our passions and true feelings.

Sometimes, it is necessary to wear a mask, and we often may censor ourselves for good reasons out of respect and consideration for others. However, the problem starts when we forget to take off the mask and start to believe it is who we are. Finding safe places to express our true passions and emotions is essential to self-discovery.

Having struggled through my own drug abuse and having watched friends and clients do the same, I truly believe that drug addiction comes from an urge to escape intolerable emotions and compensate for a lack of connection. When we "mask up" and don't deal with or acknowledge uncomfortable feelings, they just continue to get worse. As our problems and addictions grow, so does the shame of acknowledging our fears and insecurities, and the tighter we hold onto the mask. I have seen many full-blown alcoholics and addicts whose lives were falling apart struggle to admit they had a problem. I remember seeing a meme a while ago where a dog was in a house that was on fire, and he was saying, "This is fine."

If our house is on fire, we need to call the fire department. Likewise, if our lives have become unmanageable, we need to ask for help.

Questions:

1. What is underneath your mask? Who are you when no one is around?

2. What are your values? What in life is most important to you?

3. In what ways do you compromise yourself for others?

4. What parts of yourself do you hide from others?

CHAPTER 5
ANGER MANAGEMENT

STEVEN

About this same time in his life, Matt and I had the following conflict where I said to him, "Hey Matt, I need you to go back and do the vacuuming downstairs again. It was a sloppy job."

"I already did it!" Matt replied angrily.

"Sorry, but you need to do it again."

At this point, Matt was posting up on me in a threatening manner. He was a fiery, 13-year-old redhead whose emotions would spin up to a fever pitch with the heat of puberty quickly and with little provocation. I didn't back down, and I continued to restate my directive to redo the vacuuming chore, while Matthew continued to escalate and repeat himself saying, "I already did it!"

Suddenly, out of nowhere, Matt swung as hard as he could and smacked his fist into my jaw, putting the full force of his body and his shoulder into the blow. For a moment, I just stood there and I was stunned. I wasn't concerned about the physical pain, but the emotional impact was overwhelming. I hadn't expected it. I had never imagined our relationship would come to this, and some part of me was heartbroken. I didn't consider for even a moment that hitting him back was an option, but we did have to give him consequences and restrictions after this happened. There was a tiny cut on my jaw where he hit me, but it was really just a scratch. Matthew's hand, however, had a long cut on his knuckles from hitting my face and he needed stitches.

A few hours later, we were in the ER and the doctor was examining Mathew's hand to give him stitches. I saw the doctor look at Matthew's hand and look at the small cut on my face. I watched the doctor slowly scan the rest of Matthew, looking for bruises that might have come from any retaliation from me. I was silently grateful that I had never retaliated, because I knew the doctor was a mandated reporter who would have to report me to Human Services if I had struck Matthew back. After this incident, we took Matt to a counselor who diagnosed him with Mood Disorder, Unspecified. The counselor told us that this basically meant Matthew had high impulsivity and low frustration tolerance.

The memory of that incident haunted me for a long time afterward. I wondered where I had gone wrong, and what I had done to get our relationship to this point. Like many parents, I felt shame for all my many faults as a human being that may have contributed to this situation. Many nights I laid awake, worrying about my son and about our family relationships.

Certain redheads are known for their anger, aggression, and impulsive behavior which can be a gift and a curse. Cuchulainn (pronounced koo chu layn), also named the Hound of Ulster, is the archetype of the fiery redhead warrior of Celtic lore that would lash out at others impulsively. Cuchulainn, a demigod who was the greatest warrior of his day, was always doing some impulsive or violent act. He was fearless, but also remorseful when his anger went too far, and this description fit Matthew perfectly during this period in his life.

While his intense emotions and fiery temperament were difficult, often times, his assertiveness, pure fearlessness and ability to go straight for what he wanted were also tremendous gifts. As Matthew has grown older and more mature, these same traits, when tempered with life experience and his hard work on self-improvement, have become social, emotional, and spiritual gifts that are quite impressive.

MATTHEW

My dad and I are very strong-willed, and growing up we fought a lot. Neither one of us wanted to back down. One night, my dad had asked me to vacuum and I didn't want to do it, so I did a half-assed job. He told me to do it again and I said no, refusing to back down. At this point, it wasn't even about vacuuming. It was about some distorted unreasonable pride.

The next thing I knew, I was throwing a punch at my dad. As soon as my fist landed, I knew I had gone too far. My hand was bleeding, and there was an incredibly shocked expression on my dad's face. I washed my hands in the bathroom and started crying. I remember feeling scared and out of control. What was wrong with me? We drove to the hospital and I had to get several stitches in my hand.

Lesson: True conflict resolution requires us to let go of "being right."

There is a Doctor Suess book called *The Zax*. Zax are imaginary creatures that only walk in one direction. Two Zax, one going north and one going south, run into each other. They both refuse to move, and eventually an entire city is built around them. My dad and I have been a bit like the Zax. We both will refuse to move once we find our hill to die on.

Many times in life, stubbornness and an unwillingness to concede any ground can damage relationships. Sometimes, we have to be the first person to offer the olive branch of peace. Being flexible does not mean being weak. A willow will bend and survive the storm, while a heavy oak will break. It is not that there aren't any causes worth fighting for, or that we should never stand up for ourselves, however we need to learn the difference between setting a healthy boundary and being run by our ego and pride. Many of the disagreements in our lives share certain patterns. We tend to recreate the same dispute with different people, and take on the same roles in the conflict cycle.

Negative, unproductive styles of conflict include competing, avoiding and accommodating. Competing is when both parties refuse to budge on a "my way or the highway" kind of approach. This can lead to escalation as both individuals match each other's rising aggression, trying to dominate the conversation. This is the most destructive kind of conflict, and at times will lead to personal attacks, and even physical altercations.

Avoidance is pretty self-explanatory. When someone continually avoids conflict because it makes them uneasy or they just "don't like drama," it leads to a collapse in effective communication as problems are never dealt with until they become too big to avoid.

The accommodating style of conflict is suppressing our opinions and thoughts, giving into others' demands in order to end the argument. Like avoidance, this style is also common in people that dislike conflict and confrontation. What these styles have in common is that differences are never reconciled, and someone's needs generally aren't being met. More productive styles of conflict resolution take the needs of both people, and the solution is somewhere in the middle.

Questions:

1. In what ways does stubbornness and pride show up in your life?

2. Would it be helpful to be more flexible or try and understand the other person's perspective in these situations?

3. What are some ways you could be more flexible moving forward?

4. What has been the impact of negative conflict in your life?

5. What are some things you could do to improve conflict in your life?

CHAPTER 6
THE FIGHT

MATTHEW

When I was in 8th grade, I was in full swing of my rebellion and drug use. The only thing my friends and I did together was use drugs, and I was very miserable and failing school. I started to develop a bit of a reputation. I was regularly called into the principal's office after other kids reported my buddies and me smoking weed and cigarettes by the local skate park. A part of me relished the new persona, and I also felt incredibly lonely. Bryan, one of the kids in my class, made a habit of making fun of my companions and me. Looking back, I'm sure he had his own insecurities and trauma, but at the time, I really only saw him as a bully. I was hanging out with a few friends, and we were all commiserating about the way he had been treating us. One said I should fight him. "Come on man, show him that he can't mess with us."

As soon as the idea had been verbalized, it caught fire. Everyone repeated, "Yeah, you should kick his ass, Matt. You could totally take him."

I puffed up a bit with my comrades' praise, but was a bit unsure. "Nah, I don't want to get in trouble."

After some mild protests, I allowed my friends to drag me over to where he and his companions were hanging out on the basketball court.

After taunting and goading on both sides, without thinking I punched him in the face.

A few of his companions helped him to the nurse's office just as the bell rang. I numbly walked to class. Everything seemed like a dream. I couldn't believe what had just happened.

About 20 minutes into class, I was called down to the office. After filling out a form describing what had happened, the school police officer opened the door. Next thing I knew, I was being handcuffed. In complete shock, I was herded down the hallway and into the back of a police car. The school had large windows in each classroom overlooking the parking lot, and I could see hundreds of other kids watching me as I was driven away in the back of the police car.

STEVEN

In the schoolyard around the corner, Matt confronted another boy and punched him in the face with a group of teens crowding around chanting, "Fight, fight, fight!" For a 13 year old, Matt was muscular and physical, and he covered up his feelings of hurt and loneliness with anger and aggression. The other kids were telling Matt to fight this guy who they said was bullying some of the weaker kids. In the 8th grade, Matthew was desperate to feel like he mattered to someone. He craved approval, and thought he could get acceptance by being a tough guy.

The other kid was bleeding profusely from his mouth. Instead of hitting Matt back, he went straight to the lunch room where the teachers saw him bleeding. The school resource officer was called, and he arrested Matt and took him away in handcuffs to the Juvenile Assessment Center (JAC). Liz and I got a call from the school, and picked up Matt from the JAC a few hours later, as soon as they allowed us to come. In his mind, Matthew was protecting his friends from a bully, but in the minds of his victim's companions and family, Matthew was the bully who was a danger to the other students, and was a potential Columbine attack waiting to happen.

Matthew had assault charges, and got probation for the next year. He also had to complete a weekend work program for three weekends, and perform 20 hours of community service. Every month, Matt had to attend the local county court to have his compliance with the terms of probation reviewed by a judge. He finished the required classes, paid his fines, and completed his community service at our church. Matt also concluded a few weekend work programs. He stayed in a cabin in the woods from Friday through Sunday with other teens, and chopped wood while wearing an orange jumpsuit, the required dress code for the weekend.

Matthew's counselor gave him a diagnosis of Mood Disorder, and described this diagnosis as essentially, "high impulsivity and low frustration tolerance." We already knew this from our interactions at home, but independent professional confirmation redirected Matthew to a special mental health court for teens that was focused on rehabilitation rather than punishment.

About halfway through his probation, we caught Matt using marijuana which was against the conditions of his release. I also knew that he had passed the court ordered UA drug screen tests. I told him that he needed to tell the judge about his marijuana use. He was angry and said I was betraying him, and that telling the judge would break his trust with me. Right before his next court appearance in the private conference room with our lawyer, I gave him the choice, "Matt, you can either tell the judge or I will."

Our lawyer was a family friend who represented us on her own time, and I was grateful to her. She told me not to tell the judge about Matt's marijuana use for legal reasons, but I was clear and stayed firm on my position. I knew Matt needed to be accountable for his choices, even if it cost him some legal consequences. I believed the outcome he would face as a teen was much smaller than the effects he'd encounter as an adult if he didn't learn these lessons at a younger age.

In the courtroom a few minutes later, Matt told the judge and the outcome was the Weekend Work Program. However, the judge thanked Matt for his honesty. I told Matt that earning the trust of the judge was more important than these short-term problems. Years later, Matt told me that he didn't trust me again until he was almost twenty, about seven years later.

Through this process, Matt ultimately completed all his court conditions, and he learned some long-term lessons of honesty and integrity that have stayed with him to this day. This was a very painful chapter of our family lives, and I am incredibly grateful for the bonds of family and friends that supported us. Since that time, Matt has grown into a remarkable human being. He still is fearless and stands up for what he believes, but now channels his passionate nature into a commitment for a better world.

Lesson: Setting healthy interpersonal boundaries.

We are often afraid to set boundaries, especially toward the people we love, because we feel we might damage the relationship or seem to be controlling. However, boundaries are actually an expression of how much we value the relationship and love the other person. We are not only taking care of ourselves, but also caring for the other person. It does not help someone to let them get away with negative behaviors. Culturally, we often equate love with giving people what they want, but that does not build authentic relationships. If we are not honest with someone about the impact of their actions, they will not have the opportunity to learn from their mistakes. We will be left feeling violated and bitter, and it will come out in the relationship in other negative ways. Setting healthy boundaries takes a lot of patience, empathy, courage and wisdom.

First, we need to genuinely ask if there is anything in the situation that we can own ourselves. Taking accountability for our part helps "disarm" the other person, and they will more likely listen to us. Next, we must be very clear and firm with the boundary we are setting, leaving nothing up for interpretation or wiggle room. Finally, we have to continuously hold our boundaries. We are creatures of habit, and even if someone has the best intentions, it can be easy to fall into old habits. We can still be loving and compassionate as we firmly hold our ground.

Questions

1. What are some situations in your life that you feel a boundary you have has been crossed or not communicated?

2. What gets in the way of you communicating honestly about your boundaries?

3. Create a plan for a boundary you want to hold. What is the situation? What is the boundary? (It is important to define it in clear terms.) What is the best way for you to communicate this boundary? (Practice this conversation with before having it.)

CHAPTER 7
BROKEN MASCULINITY

MATTHEW

When I was a freshman in high school, I joined the football team. My two best friends were on it and I was excited to play and make new friends. What I quickly found was that being successful on and off the field in the football culture meant learning how to "be a man." That apparently involved getting back on the field, even if you were confused or didn't know what to do. It meant dominating everyone weaker than you, boasting of your sexual exploits, and not showing emotion.

This mentality was reinforced by statements often repeated by our coaches and older players like, "Don't be a pussy," "Stop crying and start playing," "Bros before hoes," and similar statements. It also discouraged any non-masculine intimacy. These dysfunctional beliefs held me back for years from love, intimacy, trust and relationships.

A few years ago, I was leading a group on masculinity at the treatment center where I worked, and was sharing these concepts. After I got through my introduction about how broken masculinity can contribute to addiction, Daniel, one of the guys in the group, said things like, "Sometimes you just need to be a man," and "The world won't cut you any breaks because you're vulnerable." He explained that these were the values he was instilling in his son because he didn't want him to get beat up, and he wanted him to be successful. I took his comments in stride, thanked him for sharing, and then got back to facilitating the group. A lot of other men shared how their ideas about masculinity had damaged their relationships, and in a lot of ways led to their addiction.

About halfway through the workshop, Daniel started crying. When there was a pause in the conversation, he spoke up and said, "Holy shit, I've been raising my son to be just like me. I don't want him to be in rehab at 40." He went on to share about his dad's lack of empathy and how being in the military had made him feel unsafe and uncomfortable with sharing his problems and emotions. Even now, he was ashamed to talk about his addiction to alcohol and cocaine. He looked at me fervently, "This needs to stop, I can't let my son end up like me."

Lesson: A more mature definition of manhood.

From a very young age, men are conditioned to behave in a very narrow definition of cultural masculinity. Some common ideas of what it means to be a man are to be strong, don't ask for help, don't cry, don't show too much affection toward friends, partners and children, be the breadwinner, and take on all of the responsibility for keeping the family safe and supported. The result is men who are afraid to show emotion, who suffer silently, and who avoid intimacy. This can result in very negative coping strategies like drug or alcohol abuse, violent behavior, and even suicide. Of course, this is not a hard rule, but is something many men and boys (myself included) have experienced.

Being open and vulnerable, healing trauma, sharing our thoughts and emotions, and finding strong supportive intimate relationships is incredibly important to leading a life full of love and intimacy. In order to live a fulfilling life, a lot of men must first break down these walls and redefine themselves as husbands, fathers, brothers, friends, and men before they are truly able to find true intimacy and happiness.

Women are just as impacted by cultural narratives as men. Some ideals in our culture about what it means to be the "perfect" woman are to be polite, even if it means not speaking up for themselves, always looking good, and meeting the needs of the people around them, even at personal expense.

Questions:

1. What are the stories you have about the role you are supposed to play as your gender?

2. What has been the impact of these stories in your life?

3. What are ways you could break out of societal stories about who you should be and how you should act and live more authentically?

CHAPTER 8
CODEPENDENCY AND RELATIONSHIPS

MATTHEW

My first major relationship was with a girl who had just gotten out of a Wilderness Treatment Program for alcohol and cocaine addiction. This was honestly the first time I had been so close and intimate with someone, and I was absolutely in love. She was open about being in recovery, and was an incredibly vibrant and intelligent girl. When my parents met her, she was completely transparent about where she was in her life, and we all had a great conversation about wanting to support her as a family.

Moving forward into the relationship, I started noticing little things. Stories I heard from her and from friends didn't add up. We lived very close and had many mutual friends, and I would hear about her sleeping with someone else. She would convince me that my peers just wanted to make me jealous and sabotage our relationship. Instead of seeing her as she was, I saw what I wanted to see.

It got to the point where I doubted our conversations, questioning things I saw and heard with my own eyes and ears. It reached a breaking point when she and my family went out to dinner for my mom's birthday. She looked pale, and there were dark circles under her eyes. When we first started dating, she was very outgoing, kind, and respectful toward me and my family. She was the complete opposite during this car ride, acting very rude to my parents. At one point, my dad looked at her through the rear view mirror and asked her calmly if she was using drugs again. She went dead silent, and was on her phone the rest of the car ride. Dad told her we could sit down and have an honest conversation about what was going on or he would take her home.

We arrived at the restaurant, and she got out of the car and walked away. Like a lost puppy, I followed her. "Hey, my dad means well. I think we're all just worried about you. Can we just go back and talk to my parents?"

"Your mom and dad are such condescending assholes," she replied. "I don't want to hear it; I have enough unsupportive people in my life that don't trust me."

I pleaded with her to stay, and told her what I thought she wanted to hear. I said I believed her, rather than being honest that I was scared of her relapsing. I just didn't want her to leave. In my own way, I was trying to manipulate her.

My dad said he would take her home, and we both rode back together to her house. I kissed her goodbye, and said I would call her. On the way back to the restaurant, I angrily asked, "What the fuck, Dad, why did you do that?"

"Matthew, she is obviously still using and lying to us about it. I don't want that around our family."

I thought back to all the conversations that didn't add up, the way she looked, and the things I'd heard from my friends. I suddenly realized how obvious it was, and that my dad was right.

"I guess you're right," I said. At that moment, I realized how selfish I had been. I hadn't wanted to confront her about it because I thought I couldn't be happy without her, and if I was honest, I would lose her. I realized at that moment I hadn't really loved her; I just loved the way she made me feel. I thought about what a bright, intelligent, and beautiful person she was. I thought about how much she could accomplish with her life if she wasn't trapped by drug use. I thought about how horrible it was that her addiction took away the parts of her I had come to cherish and admire. I started crying. "I feel so fucking helpless, Dad."

"I know," he replied, "but she has to decide that she wants help."

That moment was the first time I truly loved her unconditionally, without needing her to make me feel whole. At that instant, I experienced the clarity of my own wholeness within myself. I had a phone call with her later in the week and confronted her about the drugs and the lying. She admitted she had been using and told me she didn't want to stop. I told her my parents could help her get treatment, and she said she didn't need help. At that point, I knew the best thing for both of us was to break up. I told her I'd love to be in her life and support her when she decided to get clean.

STEVEN

Two weeks into his new relationship, Matthew told us that his girlfriend had just been released from rehab. We were concerned, but ultimately who he dated was his own choice and we wanted to be supportive. After some discussion, we agreed to come together at a local pizza place to meet her and talk more. Andrea was beautiful, smart and funny. She took accountability for her history of substance abuse, and we even talked about the warning signs to look for if she started to fall off the wagon. She stated that she was in a much better place and affirmed her commitment to staying sober. After the meeting, Liz and I felt much better about the whole situation and we thanked Andrea for agreeing to talk with us.

Everything seemed to be going okay until about a month later. We were on a trip to Florida to attend my niece's wedding, and on the trip, Matthew was looking more distracted, worried and upset. When I asked him what was going on, he told me that he was concerned because he kept seeing Andrea on social media at parties hanging out with a sketchy crowd. Throughout the trip, Matthew got worse, and he started crying at times and looked anxious and confused. He missed most of the family events on the trip, and he was on the phone a lot with Andrea. She kept reassuring him that everything was fine, but the evidence on social media kept piling up and Matt started sharing his concerns that Andrea was hanging out with an old boyfriend.

Shortly after we got home from the trip, we went out to a Japanese steak house for Liz's birthday and Matthew brought Andrea. We were driving to the restaurant, and Matt and Andrea were arguing in the third-row seat of the minivan. Apparently, Matthew had caught Andrea in a lie and she was denying any wrongdoing, taunting Matt and laughing at him. Later, Matt told me they had spoken on the phone for an hour the previous day. She said it was not her on the phone, but it was her sister, and they sometimes pretended to be each other. Matt was getting more and more confused and upset, and Andrea was derisive and edgy in her taunting of him.

As a counselor, I have seen the impact of addiction many times where the people around the addict are constantly questioning themselves and confused about the addict's lies. In that moment, this situation looked familiar. I watched in the rear view mirror while we were stopped at a red light, and asked in a quiet voice, "Andrea, are you still sober?"

She looked at me and said nothing. She completely ignored me the rest of the night, and when we got to the Japanese steak house, she and Matt promptly went outside to continue their tense conversation. After about five minutes of sitting at the restaurant, I said to Liz and our other boys, "Sorry, but I can't do this," and I got up to find Matt and Andrea. They were sitting on the grass behind the restaurant and I went up to them and said, "Sorry guys, but I need to take Andrea home." Matt, Andrea and I got in the car and I told Liz we would be back to pick them up after we dropped Andrea off at home.

She still didn't talk to me or make any eye contact as we got in the car and drove her home, but as we were driving, Matt confronted me saying, "Dad, don't be a counselor. You don't know what's going on!"

I didn't engage with Matt until we dropped off Andrea at her mom's house. When we were alone, Matt started expressing his doubts about Andrea's behavior and became more upset and anxious. When we all got home, Liz and I sat on our bed with Matthew, and he broke down and cried with deep wrenching sobs. He said that he had seen Andrea on social media, hanging out with a sketchy crowd and having fun with her old boyfriend at parties. She kept dismissing it, saying it was nothing. At that point, Liz and I encouraged Matt to cut her off and not see her anymore, and he agreed. As parents, we knew that if we had told him not to see her before he was ready, it could make him want to see her more. We had waited for the right time, and this was it.

A few weeks later, we were getting in the car at our local library. I saw Andrea standing across the parking lot just staring at Matt, trying to get his attention. I nudged Matt and nodded over to Andrea. He looked back and saw her, then turned to me and said, "Let's go, Dad," as he continued to get in the car. When we drove away, he never looked at her or even glanced back. That's when I knew he was finally getting over her, and I was grateful he was learning some powerful life lessons.

Lesson: Seeing people for who they really are.

This relationship taught me a lot. I realized I could care about and love people, even if they wanted nothing to do with me. I learned how to set boundaries, how to ask for help, and how to try a little harder to get to know people as they truly are.

What I had thought was love, and what many of us mistake love to be, was infatuation or codependency. We are mesmerized by someone's looks, or the way they make us feel. Some very important and valid human needs are love, affection and relationship. The strongest cultural story for fulfilling these needs is falling in love with the "one." The knight rescues the princess and they live happily ever after. While falling in love is an incredibly important part of life, it often fails to meet our expectations. When we realize the person we've fallen in love with is just as human as the rest of us, and is not capable of meeting all of our needs, relationships often fall back on codependent and manipulative behavior. The truth is that one person cannot be a substitute for good friends, a meaningful career, a supportive community or self-acceptance.

In my mind, true love is really seeing someone for who they are, and asking what they truly need. Through the media and from cultural stereotypes, we are inundated with what a perfect relationship should look like from a young age, and told that true love is the answer to all of our problems. We often project our idea of a perfect partner onto someone, and fail to see them more realistically. I was a very lonely teenager who didn't have a lot of friends. I had poor feelings of self-worth, and I craved love and intimacy. I saw this relationship as my one lifeline and went to incredible lengths of self-deception to preserve it.

We often try so hard to make our partners into perfect caretakers, cheerleaders, therapists and roommates. When unexamined and unmet, our unconscious need for love and acceptance is so strong that we believe the perfect partner can make up for the hole inside of ourselves. This is the definition of codependency. Rather than being codependent, we should aim to be interdependent. Interdependence means having a strong sense of identity and self-worth. Then, from that base, we are able to healthfully enter into a relationship that is about mutual trust, respect and growth. Partners that are interdependent have clear communication, strong boundaries, and do not seek to meet all of their needs from each other.

Lesson: Love is letting go.

A while ago, a friend told me something very beautiful about his relationship with his wife. He said that when they started dating, they sat down and created visions for their lives. He told me that he did not want the vision he had for his life to interfere at any point with the vision she had for hers. If we truly love someone, we are able to ask if the relationship is truly in their best interest. When we allow ourselves to enter a relationship as a playful dance, rather than a serious contract, we are able to avoid trying to force the other person to change to meet our needs. We have enough self-respect to not let them do that to us even though they may try.

How does someone protect a butterfly? Of course, the answer is to set it free. If we try to put it in a cage or control it in some manner, even with good intentions, it will only harm this tender creature. So many times in our lives, we try to control other people or situations because we think we know what's best. What often happens, is we simply create unnecessary conflicts that complicate the relationship. Often, the best way for a relationship or situation to heal is to let it be, allowing it to unfold and let others live their lives as they see fit. If they want our advice or help, they will ask for it.

In the Native American culture, the butterfly is a symbol of transformation because of the process of change from caterpillar to winged flight. We can have this type of transformation when we are willing to let go of control, releasing our ideas of how we think the problem should be solved, and entering into a partnership with the flow of life. We can accept that a higher purpose is being fulfilled when we trust the process and come from a loving place of clarity rather than frantically trying to control the situation.

We must learn to release our fear and let go of control. Trust the process. When we dance with the flow of our life situations, and are lovingly responsive to the events in our lives, we will be amazed at what can happen.

Questions:

1. How would you describe your current relationships in life? (It doesn't have to be just with your significant other.) Are they built around mutual growth or trying to meet unmet needs?

2. What are the patterns of conflict and conflict avoidance in your relationships?

3. What are several ways you compromise yourself in your current relationships?

4. How could you start to build more patterns of interdependence in your life?

CHAPTER 9

WHEREVER WE GO, THERE WE ARE

MATTHEW

Eventually, I was able to get clean at 18. I was tired of being miserable, feeling like shit all the time, and hating myself. I started getting into yoga and meditation, and did a 200-hour yoga teacher training. It was a really positive experience for me, and I was the only guy in a group of about 20. Being surrounded by so many beautiful, spiritual, and intelligent women was amazing. I was far from the "player" I thought I was, and ended up being the "little brother" of the group. I got a lot of helpful and worthwhile platonic attention and affection. We often did eye gazing, group hugs and partner yoga, and. it was a healing experience for me. After completing my training, I worked a couple of odd jobs, and one day found a Teaching English as a Foreign Language (TEFL) program in Costa Rica. Their website was filled with beautiful beaches, oceans, and joyful people. It seemed like an incredible adventure. I took English teaching (TEFL) classes during the day and taught at night. It was wonderful to learn the local culture and meet some really amazing people. After finishing the course, I enrolled in a Spanish immersion program and started living at a local hostel. The hostel was called Las Mariposas, "the butterflies." It was owned by a German woman and run by a very eccentric (and usually very drunk) man from Argentina named Hernando. He was extremely welcoming and called everyone who visited the hostel, "my big family."

Every night, he would ask all of us for help cooking, and we all pitched in to create an amazing dinner. I met people from all over the world and made some very close friends. However, I always had a feeling I was running from myself. I still struggled with depression and self-worth, and found that even among beautiful people and places, I could not fill the hole inside of me. I remember talking with a friend from America who also struggled with depression, saying, "You know, here I am, in one of the most beautiful places in the world, surrounded by all of these amazing people, and I still feel like plain old depressed me." Despite having some wonderful times, and making amazing friends, I still often felt like that.

Lesson: Happiness comes from within.

We often feel happiness is to be found out there – on some exotic beach, in the arms of a beautiful person, in a bottle, pill, or in some product. However, wherever we go, there we are. I am extremely grateful for all my encounters traveling and meeting people. Yet, the most profound occurrences for me have been traveling my inner landscape. While traveling, seeing beautiful places, and having fun experiences are an important part of life, they can become another form of escape. Bhutan is one of the happiest countries in the world, but most people there would be considered extremely below the poverty line in the U.S.

What they lack in material wealth, they make up for in a strong culture, community, and spiritual tradition. In the first world, it is often easy to compare ourselves to others or wish we were somewhere else. We are constantly shown images of attractive people having fun and amazing experiences, and sold messages about how much better life would be if we had more money, were smarter, had better looks, or a bigger house. The result is that we feel inadequate and don't value what we have. In wishing that we were somewhere else, or someone else, we miss out on how amazing the ordinary moments of our lives can be. Nowadays, I am far happier on the phone with a friend or having lunch with my mom than when I was traveling. Although sometimes, we need to leave where we are to realize what we have. Gratitude is one of the most effective ways to be more joyful. Studies have shown that writing down what we are grateful for just once a day can make people happier and reduce symptoms of depression. [1]

Questions

1. What are ways you compare yourself to others or wish your life was different?

2. Does this impact your ability to enjoy and be present in your life? If so, how?

3. What are you the most grateful for in your life? Be specific.

4. What people in your life have made the largest impact? How would your life be different without them?

---

[1] https://wanderersway.com/blogs/wanderers-way/the-science-behind-gratitude-journaling

CHAPTER 10
FINDING PASSIONS AND FACING FEARS

MATTHEW

After my experience in Costa Rica, I churned through many odd jobs, took some community college classes, and kept working on myself. While I was definitely a lot happier than when I had been using substances, I still felt a bit lost. I struggled to make friends and felt something was missing. I didn't feel like I was accomplishing much or doing anyone much good. I still had a lot of anger toward the world, and felt very helpless to create the changes I wanted to see.

My parents encouraged me to enroll in school full-time and I resisted because I was really anxious about the cost of going to school. Eventually, they convinced me to go to an information session for Colorado Mountain College. The slideshow was of a bunch of college students backpacking, taking water samples, and having adventures in the mountains. Several alumni came and talked about their experiences, sharing what an amazing impact the school had on their lives. Class sizes were small, and the teachers took personal time to get to know and build relationships with students. Also, I could go rock climbing and backpacking for class! To me, this seemed amazing. My idea of school was sitting in a room with buzzing fluorescent lights and staring at the clock. I agreed to apply, and when I got in, I decided maybe this was just what I needed.

I still struggled socially and had a hard time making friends the first couple of weeks. I eventually found a really quirky and fun group of peers. We were all a bit awkward and nerdy, and it felt a bit like I had found my way to the island of misfit toys, where we all had our own defects, but still loved each other through them. Outdoor Education and Sustainability quickly became my two favorite subjects. I went on a lot of amazing trips in my Outdoor Education classes and really developed my relationship with nature. I felt my appreciation for the wilderness grow with each trip we took. Being able to find a deeper connection with the world helped show me how much larger the world was, and how much I personally had to offer it.

While taking these amazing Outdoor Education courses and deepening my appreciation and connection to the wilderness, I learned more about the damage society is causing to nature. It brought into question my entire worldview and personal values. How could I have such a profound appreciation for the natural world, and justify a lifestyle that seemed to be destroying it? I wrestled with intense feelings of dread, grief, anger, guilt and despair.

That year also happened to host a record number of heat waves and wildfires. For months, I could see clouds of smoke covering the sky by my college. The internal fear I was holding was given a physical shape. I fell into a deep depression; my grades fell, relationships suffered, and I struggled to make it to class.

One of my professors helped me get through everything I was feeling. He was the head of the Outdoor Department and taught a lot of environmental classes as well. His Environmental Ethics class in particular had a huge impact one me. He wove a fascinating narrative about the birth and struggles of the environmental movement and everything it had overcome. Fifty years ago, there wasn't even a debate on whether businesses should be held accountable for pollution. Now companies are regularly called out for environmentally destructive practices. He was honest about the challenges we all faced, but also had an incorrigible and contagious sense of hope and optimism in the potential of human beings. One thing he said to us that I won't forget was, "If you leave this class with a sense of hopelessness, then I have not done my job. There is no point in gaining knowledge if it does not lead to action."

Throughout the years, even as the climate has continued to worsen, I have found a stronger foundation of hope and acceptance within myself. I realized that the more I put my focus on the people I care about and the things I have control over, the more I accomplish and the more my influence grows.

Lesson: Creating change from a place of love and passion.

When striving to create positive change in the world, it is easy to get discouraged when we often see the opposite of what we want happening. Helplessness and despair come from emotional numbing, and we are all faced with an enormous amount of pain that we can do nothing about on a daily basis.

In this day and age, we are constantly bombarded with the plight of others. Whether it's starving children in Africa, war refugees, suicides in our local communities, or even just the pain and angst that people in our own lives are experiencing, we often can't help but feel for others. This constant information overload can numb and desensitize us. It can put us in a constant state of fear and anxiety, where we are too overwhelmed to actually do anything helpful. In the midst of this, I think a much more important question to ask than "What are we afraid of?" is "What do we love?" Action is so much more powerful when it comes from love rather than fear.

How do we retain an open heart for others and the world without becoming paralyzed by the sheer enormity of the amount of suffering on the planet? For me, a good first step is acceptance. In Buddhism, one of the principles is that suffering is inherent to life. This doesn't mean we shouldn't work toward alleviating our suffering or that of others, but the fact of the matter is that as long as there is life on earth, there will be suffering. In accepting this, we can begin moving forward. We can let go of our resistance to reality, and move toward working with it. Being a sensitive and empathetic individual, another way I've found to handle feeling overwhelmed is learning to embrace discomfort rather than trying to escape it.

The more I increase my tolerance for hard situations, difficult emotions and conflict, the better I am able to handle them. However, sometimes it is important to just take a step back from everything. I remember getting really worked up and stressed about the election in 2016. I was having panic attacks in class on a regular basis. Being in a constant state of despair and angst only served to exhaust me mentally. It made me ineffective in my life and hard to be around. I spent a couple weekends at my parents' house, meditating and walking my dog. I came back to my life refreshed and more mentally and emotionally prepared to face what was going on. The main point I am trying to make is, it is important to be aware of what's going on around us and in the world, but it is easy to get caught up in everything and let it tear us down mentally and emotionally. It's not about completely turning away from the world, but rather taking care of ourselves so we can be of service to others.

In order to find a deeper source of passion and motivation, we must not allow ourselves to be shut down in the face of adversity. We must learn to express our pain for the world, and mourn our losses within a community of understanding and compassion. Then we will find strength and motivation we never knew we had.

> **"Unless someone like you cares a whole awful lot, nothing is going to get better, it's not."**
>
> **– The Lorax**

Questions:

1. What problems in the world are you passionate about?

2. What stops you from following your passions?

3. What are some actions you could take to support the kind of world in which you want to live?

CHAPTER 11
LESSONS IN THE HOT SPRINGS

One of my English professors in college was very eccentric. An assignment she gave us was to watch people in public for a few hours and write down our observations. When the teacher gave me this assignment, I was a little nervous. My first thought was, "She wants us to stalk other people for class? I might just take a zero on this one!" Eventually, I decided to just do it. My friend and I went to Glenwood Hot Springs one night. I realized it was as good a time as any to get my assignment over with, and people might not notice me staring through the steam. The smoke smelled slightly sulfurous, but it was well worth it to bask in the cool, calming, caring waters and collect my thoughts. The steam curled lazily around us, timidly approaching us, then retreating. The other people around us pressed close together, deep into their particular brand of gossip. A light babbling creek washed over me. One couple splashed each other happily. Another bickered quietly, but in more of a familiar and comfortable than angry tone. The whole time the moon shone softly down on us.

It was getting late, the constant chatter dying down, while my companion and I sat together in silence. I comfortably caressed the water, carefully making cool patterns with my fingers. I felt blessed, being able to relax in the hot springs, grateful for the company of my friend, and happy to stare at the moon and stars. The past week had been a whirlwind of confusion and anxiety, and it was simply amazing to let all the stress wash off of me. Finally, after having a deep conversation about the metaphysical and philosophical meanings of Star Wars, we decided it was time to leave. When we got back to the dorms, I said good night, and lay back in my bed, still feeling like I was floating. Sometimes, we all need a little self-care and reflection. From the time I got to the hot springs to when I left, I could see tension melt off the faces of the people around me, as their frantic minds gave in to the gentle movement and warmth of the springs. I think there's a reason human beings are drawn to hot springs. In a lot of ancient cultures, they were considered sacred, and the pinnacle of luxury in Roman and Greek society. A lot of life is stressful, and it's almost a religious experience to cleanse ourselves of it every once in a while.

Lesson: Taking time for self-care.

Our culture can be so fast-paced, we often forget to relax and take care of ourselves. We are expected to always be available, and can barely find any time away from the stresses of daily life. When we don't allow ourselves to have a break, stress can build up. As humans, we are not designed to stay stressed for long periods of time. This can result in depression, anxiety, and a lot of physical problems. We also are more creative when we give our mind space to wonder.

Questions:

1. How much of your time do you have to spend taking care of yourself?

2. What do you already do for self-care? What have you been putting off?

3. How could you create more time for yourself during the week?

CHAPTER 12
SHARING OUR BURDENS TOGETHER

MATTHEW

One summer, a friend invited me to a sweat lodge in western Colorado. I have been going to sweat lodges and other Native American ceremonies since I was a kid, so I jumped at the chance. After a long drive, I pulled up in the driveway. As soon as I knocked on the door, a serene, but average looking old man opened it. He told me his name was John. He welcomed me in and asked me to make myself at home.

After some pleasantries, we sat facing each other on his two couches. "So, how did you get into running sweat lodges and ceremonies?" I asked. He told me he had trained under a Comanche medicine man for a couple years and had been given permission to hold ceremonies. "What has been the most profound thing that you have learned from running ceremonies?"

"Well," he started, "it's definitely made me less of an asshole. I came back from Vietnam a very hard and broken man." He continued, "Being in the war made me shut down a lot and I had trouble having much of a relationship with anyone, or connecting to people in general. This way of life has helped me work through a lot of my trauma from war and my childhood, and ultimately become a better, softer man. It has shown me the truth of things and given me a window to talk to God, Spirit, the Universe, whatever you want to call it, which I think is where all healing ultimately comes from."

After talking a while longer, he took me out back and showed me around his property. It was a beautiful, heavily wooded couple of acres with a stream running through it. He had some raspberry bushes growing in a fenced-off section, and a couple of huge willow trees dominated the landscape. The sweat lodge was shaped like a dome and covered with heavy canvas. There was a half moon shaped fire pit next to it made out of rocks, and a mound of dirt in the middle that served as an altar. We spent a couple hours gathering wood until my friend and her partner arrived.

Lyn, who would look more at home at a punk concert than at a sweat lodge, walked up and gave me a hug. After some introductions and small talk, we all got to work building the fire. There is a lot of ceremony and tradition around setting up a sweat lodge. When the wood for the fire is set up, prayers are offered in each direction with tobacco, then it is scattered onto the wood. One by one, each person places a rock on top of the pile of wood. First in the East, then the South, the West and finally the North. Each direction signifies a sacred phase of life. The East represents birth and childhood, the South suggests adolescence, the West implies adulthood, and the North stands for old age and death. This is repeated until 40 rocks have been placed on the fire. Then, the fire is lit in each of the four directions.

After the rocks had been heating for about two hours, we were ready to go into the sweat lodge. I had been given the role of fire keeper, so I stayed outside of the lodge while everyone crawled in. I then brought in 14 rocks for the first round. Each rock I added was sprinkled with cedar and prayed over. After I put in the last rock, I crawled into the lodge. The door was built low to the ground, so to get in we had to get on our hands and knees. In the minds of the Native Americans, this was to humble ourselves before the Creator.

John poured several ladles of water on the fire. Hot steam immediately burst up. He then led us in singing several Lakota and Comanche songs while pounding on a drum. The steady rhythm of his voice and the drum helped keep me present through the discomfort of the steam and the rising nausea in my chest.

There was a certain primal joy in sharing in the ritual and discomfort of the experience with the people around me. As the drum and our voices reached a crescendo, and the heat was getting almost unbearable, John asked me to open the door. Walking out into the sun, I felt as if I had shed layers of negativity and I was a new person.

I spent a lot of time on John's property that summer, helping him maintain the land and prepare for ceremonies. I also enjoyed spending time in prayer and meditation. There was nothing to distract me from myself or the people around me. John spoke about his life experiences; some hard, some funny, and some incredibly profound. I was humbled by the joy and peace he had found in service. He said he was deeply touched by the pain of others he had seen in his life. His first inclination was to drown it out in substances, but at some point, he found that the path to his own healing was serving others. He provided an incredibly safe and gentle space for me to lay down my burdens for a while and find a little bit of peace.

One night, I was hiking with Lyn. I had been doing a lot of ceremonies, prayer and fasting, and was feeling emotionally raw. All of the sudden, I was hit with waves of anxiety. It was as if all of my underlying fears and anxieties about life had been unearthed and climbed out like ants under a rock. The biggest thing I felt was an aching loneliness. I've spent a large portion of my life by myself, feeling alienated from my family and community. Over the years, I have struggled a lot with faith about any higher power or ultimate meaning in life.

I sat down and Lyn asked what was wrong. I started to cry, "Life can just be really painful and lonely sometimes." She came over and wrapped her arms around me. "I know, honey, there is so much pain in this world we all have to bear, but we don't have to do it alone." Soothed by her touch and reassurance, I felt my fears and doubts start to melt away. I remembered all the times I had received unconditional love and support from my friends and family. Times I spent in the woods feeling inseparable from the life around me. I glanced at the stars, feeling the enormity of the cosmos. I still didn't know if there was some supreme being out there watching over me, but I definitely wasn't alone.

Over time, I felt my attitude and actions toward people shift dramatically. I realized how much I'd been holding myself back from others out of fear. I was so worried about my own life, I had forgotten to take the needs and wants of the people in my life into consideration. Not that I didn't care about them, I absolutely did. I was just so wrapped up in my own fears and negative thinking, I didn't have the energy left to think about anyone but myself. I'm incredibly grateful for the time I spent with John and the lessons he taught me.

STEVEN

The little boy was only nine years old. His face was contorted in pain and his shoulders heaved up and down over and over again as sobs wracked his body, and tears streamed down his cheeks. He was sitting in a child-size wooden chair in jeans and a t-shirt as he looked at the picture he had just drawn of his father in jail behind bars. We sat in silence, and he cried for the next 30 minutes until it was time to leave. There was nothing for me to do except quietly be there with him while he cried. His father had recently been put in jail for dealing crack cocaine, and his mother had brought him in for counseling. The following week, when his mother brought him back for our next therapy session, she said gratefully, "I don't know what you did, but keep doing it because he's getting better now." In this situation, all I did was give the gift of nothing. No judgments, no expectations, and no trying to fix or make it better. Just being together, pure and simple. When this young soul was feeling his pain, all there was to do was be together. In the silence and suffering, there was a profound intimacy and an exquisite peace and unconditional love we touched together. That moment was enough to begin to heal the pain of loss and the agony of shattered hopes and dreams.

Lesson: Listening without expectation or judgment.

When we spend our time working very hard to achieve our goals, or we are so focused on the struggles in our life, we can miss the pure joy that exists in the moment. This simple joy of pure being is with us right now. But, if we are focused on our future goals or past trauma playing out in our current life situations, we are not fully present in the moment. Working toward our goals is fine, but it can become an addiction that causes us to lose sight of what is most important in life. Everything we really want is right here and right now, in the silence of eternity, that constantly surrounds us with the overwhelming embrace of pure, unconditional love. We are totally loved and accepted just as we are. There is nothing we have to do or achieve to find the happiness of this inner peace except to release our preoccupation with our concern. Spending some daily time in silence or meditation can help bring the awareness of this peace to the struggles of our daily life. If we can let go of relentless attachment to our goals for the future, release the focus on our fear, and simply bring our full presence to the stillness of the present moment, we can find more peace and love.

Lesson: Learning to share our burdens together.

It is a widely held spiritual belief that thinking ourselves to be the most important person in the world is a great cause of misery. When we are focused on our own problems and happiness, we lose sight of the concerns of others around us. Ironically, thinking only of our own happiness does not make us happier.

There is an ancient Zen story about a boy who goes to an old wise woman because he has gone through a great tragedy. She tells him to grab a handful of salt, and put it in a cup of water. He does what she asks, and walks over to her.

"Now drink," she says.

The boy spits out the water. "That was terrible!" he exclaims.

She then tells him to grab another handful of salt and follow her. Perplexed, he does as he is asked. Eventually, they come across a beautiful lake. She tells him to throw salt in the lake. "Now drink," she tells him. When he drinks the water it tastes clean and pure.

"How was it?" shes asks.

"Amazing!" the boy replies.

She explains to him, "When all we can think about is our own life and problems, it's like drinking from a small cup, and the salt of life is bitter. But, when we expand our concern to include the people and world around us, suddenly our own problems aren't so bitter and we are refreshed by communion with life."

In another story, a woman whose son has just died seeks the Buddha and asks him to bring her son back to life. He tells her to first go to every house in her village and bring back one mustard seed from a family that has not been touched by death. At each house, the woman hears the family's stories of death and grief. She comes back to the Buddha saying, "Nobody's family has not been touched by death and sorrow."

This fact does not minimize our own pain or grief, but rather puts them in a wider context. Suffering is universal, and sometimes the best we can do is just be there for each other.

Questions

1. What are your greatest sorrows and regrets in life?

2. What are the hardest things you have heard other people go through? This could be people in your life or other people you have heard about.

3. How does it feel to put your own problems in a bigger context?

CHAPTER 13
THE LIGHT SHINES IN THE DARKNESS

MATTHEW

When I was 20, I got a tattoo on my arm that said, "The light shines in the darkness and the darkness has not overcome it." The words were originally from the Old Testament, but I personally got the inspiration from reading *Man's Search for Meaning*. The author, Viktor Frankl, was a Jewish man from Austria that survived Auschwitz during WWII. He was an incredibly intelligent psychiatrist, and actually had the chance to leave Austria before the Germans invaded, but decided to stay because his family couldn't get visas.

In his book, he shares how going through Auschwitz strips someone of every bit of pretension, identity and dignity they have; it's brought out the best and the worst in people. He found that those who were able to find a sense of meaning and purpose in their suffering used their traumatic experiences to become more healed and whole. For Frankl, his meaning and purpose were thoughts about seeing his family and sharing his work with the world.

There is a passage in the book where he is working, and he knows if he stops, he will be shot. The thought crosses his mind that it might be better to give up and end his torment. In that moment, he has a visceral vision of his wife beside him, giving him strength and comfort. I read this book when I was 15, and in moments when I felt like giving up and ending everything, I thought a lot about the passage. How someone even in the worst circumstances could find beauty, faith and hope. Frankl went on to become one of the fathers of modern psychology, and his work and ideas have helped millions.

Lesson: Finding hope and faith in life's hardest moments.

We all have moments where our lives seem hopeless. I was having a conversation the other day with a friend who had been through a very traumatic experience, and had experienced grief and thoughts of suicide for months afterwards. She said, "I was having a lot of suicidal thoughts and feelings of intense grief and hopelessness. While those moments were incredibly hard, they have the ability to let us actively choose life, and with that comes renewed joy, energy and gratitude."

If we are having, or someone we know is having suicidal thoughts, we should get them help immediately. However, in our culture we tend to want to fix each other and jump to quick solutions rather than sit with the uncertainty of someone else's pain. In life, there is inevitably a lot of heartache and pain, and running away from it only makes it worse. Facing our own doubts and fears about the world and coming out on the other side gives us strength, gratitude, and hope for life that we could never have found otherwise. This is not to minimize what anyone has gone through, but it is possible to find purpose and meaning in our suffering. I think that one of the most important things to realize when we are feeling hopelessness and despair is we are not alone, and don't have to shoulder our burdens on our own.

There have been countless people in my life who I would not be here without their support.. A lot of the time, I didn't realize how much support was available for me until I reached out for it. In the Twelve Steps, the first three steps are about admitting our powerlessness over our addictions or problems, coming to believe in a higher power, and turning ourselves over to the care of that power. In my mind, this is the hardest part about the program. While not everyone reading this book is actively in or recovering from an addiction, we all have problems in our lives that we cannot solve on our own.

I am personally not religious, but the recognition that I am not alone, and I do not have to face my problems alone, is incredibly important. Admitting we are powerless does not convey we give up on changing our lives for the better. It means we give up the ideas and thought patterns that keep us stuck, repeating the same problems, over and over again. It means humbling ourselves and being willing to invite something new into our lives.

Questions:

1. What are some things in your life or in the world that make you feel hopelessness and despair?

2. What in your life gives your meaning?

3. What are some beliefs or patterns that you would like to change? How could you bring in a new perspective to them?

CHAPTER 14
WILDERNESS THERAPY

MATTHEW

After I graduated college with an associate degree, I started working for a wilderness therapy company in Utah. I was working with teenagers that had intense mental, emotional and behavioral issues, and most of them were forced by their parents to be in the program. Almost all of the staff, myself included, were pushed to the edges physically and emotionally. We were required to constantly be vigilant for kids trying to run, engage in self-harm, suicide attempts and other destructive behaviors.

Staff also got very little sleep or alone time "on trail" as we were required to constantly keep an eye on the students. The schedule was eight days on, six days off, so staff had little opportunity to process their experiences and recover. On my off days, I just wanted to hang out with friends and have a fun summer, so I pushed my experiences to the back of my mind.

The first couple of weeks, I was able to handle the stress fine. I really felt like I was making a positive impact on the kids and developing strong relationships with other staff. Around my fourth or fifth week on trail, we were backpacking and I was working with a group of kids on the autism spectrum. They were all very kind and funny, and I really enjoyed spending time with them. They had very interesting quirks, and I had to learn to dive into their world if I wanted to connect with them. I spent hours talking about toilets and Minecraft with one kid, and another was really excited I played Dungeons and Dragons, so we'd make up stories together.

One day, we were on a hike, and halfway through the day, a student collapsed. My initial shock faded, and my only focus was getting this kid help. While the lead guide stood there staring at the student, I was instantly called to action. Immediately, I rolled him onto his back and tried to get his attention. When he wasn't responding, I did a standard medical check, shining a light in his eyes and taking his vitals. Again, zero response. His eyes were rolled back into his head, his skin was very hot, and his heart rate was very high. We had to wait two terrifying hours for an ambulance to arrive, and the student had a seizure. I desperately did what I could with the resources I had.

In the back of my mind, I was legitimately afraid of him dying. I remember never having felt so grateful when he opened his eyes in the ambulance. After that experience, we called his parents and they still wanted to keep him in the program. He was rightfully freaked out by the whole situation and spent the remainder of the week trying to self-harm, commit suicide, or run from the program. I went home after that experience, wanting to forget about it. I only had a few days with my friends, so I jumped into life, and spent my whole time distracting myself.

Pretty soon it was time to go back. While I never had quite the extreme encounter as that, I continued the rest of that summer dealing with a lot of intense moments, and continued trying to distract myself on my off days. I never had a chance to process or integrate these events. Toward the end of the summer, I started feeling very depressed, numb and anxious, and I was getting night terrors as well. By the last week of work, I was emotionally and mentally checked out from my experience, and I was not present with the students at all.

I went camping with some friends a week after my seasonal contract ended and just completely broke down. It took me a few months to get back to normal, but luckily, I had a very strong support system and started seeing a therapist again. I felt very defeated and personally weak from not being able to handle the pressure of being a guide.

Lesson: Working through trauma and processing experiences.

I knew what I was getting into and had wanted to be a wilderness therapy field guide for a long time. The problem was, I wasn't taking time to recover or integrate these experiences. Many companies in the mental health field have a certain culture of martyrdom and don't provide the proper emotional support for their staff. Individuals get into it because they are very passionate about helping others, and they forget to take care of themselves. From talking to a lot of people in mental health and other challenging fields, I can see that the individuals who are able to sustain the emotional intensity are the ones that prioritize their own needs and self-care. While this may seem selfish, we can't fill someone else's cup if ours isn't full.

Some helpful practices to anyone working in mental health are setting therapy sessions, taking at least one day a week to completely unplug and do something mindful like hiking, journaling, meditation, and maintaining positive and supportive relationships. These self-care practices are incredibly important. It is very common for relationships and personal needs to get neglected by people that are very passionate about their career in mental health and tend to put their clients first. However, taking time for our own passions, relationships, and needs will make us more effective at work. Secondhand or vicarious trauma is personally experiencing trauma from someone else's experiences, and this can lead to PTSD and symptoms seen in individuals who actually do experience a traumatic situation. It is very common for anyone working in mental health or emergency first responders.

Researchers found that mental health professionals who were exposed to stories of traumatic experiences on a regular basis started having PTSD symptoms, even though they were never directly exposed to trauma. Often mental health workers and first responders are directly exposed to traumatic situations as well. Human beings have the ability to experience and feel secondhand trauma because of their empathy for others.

Many people called to the mental health field are very empathetic. While this gives them great understanding and compassion when working with clients, it also makes them vulnerable to secondhand trauma. Common effects of secondhand trauma are depression, anxiety, PTSD symptoms, burnout (a loss of passion and increased stress and anxiety at work), and excessive rumination on clients' experiences, to the point it impacts life outside of work. Finding coping tools to manage secondhand trauma is essential to maintaining a long-term career in mental health.

The Stress Response Cycle

- **Baseline:** Normal state of being. The body is designed to handle traumatic events. Problems arise when the body's stress response gets stuck or isn't allowed to be completed. Problems occur when the body gets stuck in "Fight or Flight" or "Freeze."

- **Fight or Flight:** The body is preparing to deal with a threat. It shows up as anger, fear, anxiety, panic or aggression. If someone has an overactive "flight response," they tend to avoid conflict and leave stressful situations. If they have an overactive "fight response," they often will be argumentative, stubborn, and/or physically aggressive. Being stuck in these states can lead to PTSD, anxiety and panic disorders, and problems with aggression and anger. Meditation, anger management, talk therapy, and finding a positive physical outlet help with being stuck in this state.

- **Freeze:** The body is so overwhelmed by its environment, it shuts down. This is common in traumatic events where someone is helpless and powerless to do anything. Long-term impacts are dissociation, depression, and an overall emotional numbing. Therapy, journaling, mindfulness, and getting back into a normal healthy routine (sleeping enough, eating healthy and exercising) help with being stuck in this state.

Questions:

1. What events have happened in your life that you felt unable to cope with or handle?

2. What triggers you? (something that shouldn't be a big deal, but you find yourself having an unnecessarily intense response).

3. What are some things you know that help reduce stress?

4. If you feel that you can get stuck in a stress response state (fight, flight or freeze), what are some things you could start doing that would help?

CHAPTER 15
ON THE TURNING AWAY

MATTHEW

I've been volunteering at a teen sobriety support group in Boulder for a few years, off and on. It is a really beautiful space that teaches teens in recovery about natural ways to support their brains in sobriety and find community support. At one point, I was having a conversation with a few individuals about the problems in the world. A kid looked at me with genuine fear in their eyes and said, "I really just don't see much hope for the future." The last year has been an incredibly intense time for teens in Boulder, and really everywhere. During COVID, a lot of teens either isolated themselves or got sucked back into intense partying and drug use. Several teens I've personally worked with have overdosed, and there have been a lot of losses in that community. Also, the March, 2021 shooting at a King Soopers in Boulder still has had ripple effects in that community. I regularly hear from Boulder teens who say their basic sense of safety feels threatened and violated. One individual in the group mentioned how little support she felt from her friends and family, and how the repeated tragedies in the Boulder community seemed to be driving people further into isolation. All of these teens stated they were extremely grateful to have the recovery group in their life. It's incredibly special to be part of a group that gives people a sense of safety, and the ability to freely express what they are experiencing.

Lesson: Building personal and community resilience.

In life, we all go through emotionally challenging experiences. When people and communities face repeated hardships and tragedy, something can happen called empathy fatigue. This means that we diminish our capacity to connect with others and struggle more to address the pain we are feeling.

On the other hand, I have seen so many amazing ways people have come together in crisis. Studies have found some individuals handle major life challenges and upheaval differently.[2] Emotional resilience is one's ability to navigate these events and come out stronger on the other end. Difficult experiences like the death of a loved one, divorce, or experiencing a natural disaster. The most important defining factor of how successful we are at navigating new situations and upheaval is the strength of our relationships and connections with our community.

Many studies have shown that communities which have gone through a disaster can actually strengthen social bonds and be motivated to make positive changes.[3][4] In moments of loss and heartbreak, we all have the choice to come together as a community and support each other, or turn away from one another. Pink Floyd says it well in their song, "On the Turning Away." "Don't

---

2   https://www.frontiersin.org/articles/10.3389/fpsyg.2020.00108/full
3   https://link.springer.com/article/10.1007/s40572-019-00239-3
4   https://journals.sagepub.com/doi/abs/10.1177/1086026616629794

accept that what's happening is just a case of others' suffering. Or you'll find that you're joining in the turning away."

Do we let trauma and pain diminish our capacity to love and connect, or do we let it open our hearts more? Today we are exposed to an extreme amount of violence and negative news in the media. Because human beings are highly empathetic, it is possible to develop a trauma response to events without being directly exposed, but just by seeing or hearing about it in the media. Instances of suicide, depression, and anxiety are skyrocketing and emotionally charged media coverage could be one major cause.

There is also a widespread amount of emotional numbing and dissociation happening to individuals as a natural response to the hyper levels of stress we are exposed to, making us less capable to connect and move forward from tragedies and create positive change. In today's day and age, widespread tragedies that impact entire communities, like natural disasters or mass shootings, are becoming more common. These events have the potential to further isolate communities and drive more antisocial behavior, or bring them together, making them stronger. Several studies have shown that in times of disaster, the recovery of the community was connected to the personal connections and ties in the community, and their shared sense of belonging to that community.[5]

Researchers also have found it is possible for the experience of a traumatic event to create positive long-term outcome in individuals. Some examples are greater appreciation of life, increased strengthening of close relationships, more compassion and altruism, identification of new possibilities or a purpose in life, greater

---

5 https://www.purdue.edu/newsroom/releases/2018/Q4/a-little-help-from-your-friends-is-key-to-natural-disaster-recovery,-purdue-research-study-suggests.html

awareness and utilization of personal strengths, and enhanced spiritual development and creative growth.[6] A person's emotional health before the trauma and how they respond to trauma after the event impact their recovery and growth.

The defining factor for developing PTSD and having repeating, long-term negative life experiences has a lot to do with the communal support someone receives and how they view the experience. Most cultures throughout history have had community rituals and traditions allowing community and individual grief to be expressed. Psychologically, if grief is not processed on an individual level, it can lead to emotional repression and numbness, loss of motivation, depression and anxiety, or anger and a desire to blame something or someone.

On a community level, unprocessed grief is the cause of war and violence. When two sides cannot grieve their losses and forgive each other, it can lead to generations of hatred. A good example of this is the Israel/Palestine conflict. With any tragedy and act of violence, each side becomes more entrenched in their viewpoint and bitter toward each other. Finding ways to communally express grief is essential to creating healthy communities.

Lesson: Finding our way past excessive individualism.

In Western culture, we value independence above everything else, which can be a blessing and a curse. On the curse side, this independence can lead to undervalued community, humility and connection. Human beings are wired to live in strong communities and support each other. When we don't have those strong

---

6 https://www.apa.org/monitor/2016/11/growth-trauma

bonds and connections, we're less able to handle adversity and can cope in negative ways, like resorting to drug abuse. We experience ourselves in the context of our relationships with family, friends, and those around us. Our communication profoundly impacts our thoughts and actions and our experience of ourselves.

An anthropologist who had been studying a remote African tribe for a long time played a game with a group of children from the tribe. He put a basket of fruit under a tree, and told them that they would race to the tree, and whoever got there first would get the basket of fruit for themselves. When he gave them the signal to run, the children all held hands and ran together. They then sat around the basket and ate the fruit together as a group. He asked them why they all ran together when they could have had more fruit for themselves. A young girl replied, "How can one of us be happy if all the other ones are sad?" This essential philosophy of "Ubuntu" has been summarized as, "I am because we are."

This type of thinking leads to the idea that our human nature is fundamentally relational, is linked to others, and ultimately is connected to the whole of the Universe. We experience the true nature of our soul in connection with others, and with the larger Universe around us. Beyond the perception of ourselves as an individual, is the experience of our fundamental connection or unity with all of life.

> **"Africans have a thing called Ubuntu. We believe that a person is a person through other persons. That my humanity is caught up, bound up, inextricably, with yours. When I dehumanize you, I dehumanize myself. The solitary human being is a contradiction in terms. Therefore, you seek to work for the common**

good because your humanity comes into its own in community, in belonging."

– Bishop Desmond Tutu

Steps to build emotional resilience.

1. Look at the big picture. See your own hardship in a larger context. Find or think about others that share your experiences.

2. Be careful where you place your attention. Be solutions focused. Don't ignore problems, but also don't get overwhelmed by them. Find positive aspects in your challenging situations.

3. Be vulnerable and reach out to people. Share your experiences.

4. Find a way to be of service and help others.

5. Let others' success and happiness make you happy.

6. Practice gratitude.

7. With everything you do, ask, "Is this helping or harming me?"

Questions:

1. What are some issues in your community and the world that make you feel hopeless and overwhelmed?

2. In what ways do you cut yourself off from other people and community during challenging times?

3. How could you open yourself up to more connection and support?

CHAPTER 16
CALM WITHIN THE STORM

MATTHEW

When I had been working in residential treatment for about a year, I encountered one of my most challenging clients. Mitch was actively coming off meth and heroin, and had pretty much been asleep the first few days he was in the program. I was working a night shift and was training a new co-worker. Mitch had an issue with another client I had not seen. According to the other participant, Mitch had threatened him. When I confronted Mitch, he immediately got angry and shouted, calling the other client a "god damn snitch." He continued to escalate and get louder. He told me to get his cigarettes, and he was going to have a smoke, then get out of there. We do not let participants have cigarettes because the area is an extreme fire hazard. I told him we could get him back down into town, but I could not give him a cigarette.

He grabbed a butter knife from the kitchen (all of the real knives were locked up), and threatened me. My co-workers took the other clients into another room and called the police. Mitch said he was going to break down the door where we keep participants' personal items and went downstairs. I cautiously went after him, and sat down across from the stairs. After several minutes of cursing, I heard him calmly coming up the stairs. At that moment, I felt strangely at ease. I wasn't angry at Mitch. I knew how much he had gone through, and how coming off of drugs was impacting his brain. I felt sorrow and compassion for what he was going through, and a strange curiosity for how our interaction would unfold. Mitch started yelling at me, telling me that all my company wanted was his money, and they didn't care about him.

"Mitch," I started with a small laugh, "what do you think they pay me here? I'd probably be making more at Home Depot." He continued to rant, and I spoke gently and calmly. "Yeah, this place is full of shit, isn't it? We really don't understand you. I get that it must be hard." Using active listening and remaining composed, I gave him no ammo to throw back at me, and it wasn't too long before he simmered down.

STEVEN

The teenager looked like he was about 15 years old. The gun was shaking in his hand as he held it high and pointed it at me. "Give me everything you've got!" It was two months before we were getting married. Liz and I were returning home from a graduate school class we had together. I was putting my key in the front door of my house when Liz tapped me on the shoulder to get my attention. When I turned around, I saw a guy with a gun running across the lawn with his friends, waiting in their car. Later, I heard it was gang initiation night, but at that moment, none of that mattered. Everything felt surreal, like in a dream, and initially I thought this must be some prank. The guy was standing three feet away from me with the gun pointed at my face, and I asked him if the gun was real. Upon hearing this, he waved the gun closer in my face and in an abusive and angry voice he said, "Do you want me to show you it's real?"

At that moment, I felt rage and my vision was obscured with a darkness that clouded any rational thought. I was not going to allow anyone to talk with me like that, regardless of who had the gun. Liz, seeing the tension that was building, knew that the other guy was holding the gun. She immediately stepped between us and said, "Don't worry, everything's going to be okay. We're going to give you what you need." She proceeded to give him her purse and reassured him. He looked at me, and continued to press me for my money. I took out my wallet and all I had was a dollar, so I gave it to him. He asked me if I had anything more and I told him, "No." He ran off, got in the car with his friends, and they drove away.

Lesson: Letting go of compulsive thinking and action.

Looking back, I feel a deep gratitude to Liz for her courage and willingness to put herself between me and harm without a second thought for her own safety. I'm also looking at myself, wondering why I'm so stubborn that I'd rather die than be forced to do anything against my will.

In many ways, this trait has been a gift, and in other ways, it has been a curse. This mindless reactivity has created many problems in my life where I make rash reactive decisions that impact my family and relationships. On the other hand, my uncompromising drive to follow my own path and be true to my inner guidance, regardless of the external situation, has been an incredible asset, leading me in productive directions in life.

This fierce independence is a coping strategy I developed in reaction to feeling powerless as I was growing up. It has operated somewhat mindlessly in my decision-making process throughout my life. Only in the last few years have I come to understand and consciously integrate the gifts of this compulsion, and learn some control over the mindless reactivity when others are telling me what to do. In conflict with others, I have an improved ability to look at what is most helpful in the situation. I make conscious choices about what is best, rather than mindlessly letting my rebel take over. My relationship with Liz has helped me get there. This greater self-awareness has created a new level of synergy and harmony in my personal relationships and helps me make better decisions. I'm not mindlessly reacting to my unconscious compulsions as I did in the past.

This is the gift of life experience; the ability to self reflect and understand the patterns running our lives. Then, we begin to unplug from these past patterns and live in the present moment, rather than remain unconsciously controlled by the ghosts of our past. Learning from our life experience can be the beginning of the golden years of wisdom if we are willing to reflect on our life and learn the lessons of our past. However, if we stay stuck in old patterns of thinking and behaving, we become more bitter and angry at the world for not being what we want it to be. Instead of our golden years being the age of wisdom, we become more isolated and bitter.

Our life experiences can teach us to release our fears and free our minds from the compulsions and dramas from our past, or we can clutch onto our fears and opinions, like Scrooge grasping onto a penny. We can be right about all our ideas, opinions and judgments, or we can have a life of joy that works better for us and everyone around us.

Lesson: Mirror neurons and empathy.

How we choose to show up and interact with the people around us has a huge impact on how they in turn treat us. Scientists have found we all have something called "Mirror neurons."[7] These are essentially what allow us to have empathy and understand others. They also mean that our emotional states and regulation are impacted by the people around us. For instance, if someone starts a conversation with us angry and accusatory, we are likely to respond with heightened emotions. On the other hand, it is very hard to stay angry at someone who is calm and compassionate toward us. Note that this is not always the case. We cannot assume that people will always be nice to us just because we are kind and loving. But, the way we approach conversations with individuals and treat them, has a huge impact on the quality of our relationships and on how people respond to us.

Strategies for emotional regulation and conflict resolution.

1. Try to stay calm and relaxed. If you feel you are being triggered, try some breathing techniques. Breath in for the count of four holding for two seconds, then breath out for six. Having a longer exhale than inhale activates your parasympathetic nervous system.

---

[7] https://www.apa.org/monitor/oct05/mirror

2. Before trying to get your point across, really listen to what the other person is saying and genuinely try to understand their point of view. If people feel heard and understood, they are more likely to listen to what you have to say.

3. If it feels like the conflict is unproductive, and you are not being respected or feel you are not capable of being kind and courteous, try taking a break. It is completely fine to take space to calm down in a conflict. The key is that you come back and resolve the issue at a later time.

Questions:

1. What is a consistent conflict you have with someone in your life? Feel free to write it down in as much detail as you want.

2. What emotional state does this conflict usually bring out in you and them?

3. How do you think this conflict would turn out if you approached it with a different emotional state?

4. Are there any expectations you have for yourself and others that cause you stress and disconnect you from others?

5. What would your life look like if you let go of judgments of yourself, events and other people?

CHAPTER 17
RADICAL SELF-RESPONSIBILITY

"I am the master of my fate. I am the captain of my soul."
- William Ernest Henley

MATTHEW

One of my favorite movies is *Invictus*. In it, Morgan Freeman plays Nelson Mandela, the first black president of South Africa. Apartheid was a system of black suppression and white control in South Africa that was even more brutal and violent than Jim Crow in America. In 1943, Mandela joined the African National Congress (ANC), which was a black advocacy and political group. They were seen as a major threat by the white government. In 1962, he was arrested for what would be 27 years. By all reports, the young man going into prison was angry and bitter, advocating for a violent takeover of the white government.

In prison, Mandela found peace with himself and his captors. He went to great lengths to learn about his jailers, and developed empathy and compassion for the White South Africa he had fought against. Despite being subjected to incredibly harsh and humiliating conditions, all of Mandela's prison guards reported he was nothing but kind and respectful to them. He often inquired about their personal lives in a genuine attempt to get to know them better. When Mandela was released in 1990, he was a powerful national voice for compassion and reconciliation on both sides. He went on to help end apartheid, and was elected president of South Africa in 1994. He easily could have become more angry and bitter in prison, and could have advocated for a civil war upon his release. However, he made the choice to make the best of his situation and find self-respect, peace and compassion in incredibly harsh circumstances.

Another story that shows the power of personal responsibility and taking action, even if they don't seem to matter, is the story of Rosa Parks. A famous leader of the 1960's Civil Rights Movement, Rosa Parks was a huge catalyst for change. On December 1st, 1955, she simply refused to give up her bus seat and sit at the back of the bus. Back then, this was a big deal. Black Americans in the South were expected to give up their seat on public transportation if asked by a white person. This was part of the horrendous Jim Crow laws that effectively made Black Americans into secondhand citizens.

This simple act sparked a nationwide bus boycott, and generated a huge amount of attention to the laws oppressing Black Americans. The interesting thing was that it was never Rosa Park's intention to gain media attention. She had no idea that she would change the course of history by refusing to give up her seat. When interviewed about the event, she simply said, "People always say that I didn't give up my seat because I was tired, but that isn't true. I was not tired physically, or no more tired than I usually was at the end of a working day. I was not old, although some people have an image of me being old then. I was forty-two. No, the only tired I was, was tired of giving in."

Lesson: Release blame and take responsibility for our reality.

While we may not always get the chance to choose the circumstances we are in, we always have a choice in the way we respond. When our partner is angry at us, do we lash back or hold a calm space and genuinely inquire as to what is wrong? The more we take conscious control and responsibility for our choices, outlook and actions, the more power we have to shape our future. Let go of the blame game.

Blame is all about shifting responsibility. When we blame other people or situations for our problems, we relinquish our power. While things outside of us have an impact on our life, the only person we ever have control over is ourselves. The advice, "Just do it," obviously doesn't work. If we could make ourselves change overnight, there would be no need for therapists, recovery groups or residential addiction treatment centers. However, the more we identify the areas in our lives where we do have control, the more this builds into a positive feedback loop. It gives us more confidence and willpower, leading to more positive decision-making. While someone who has an addiction to alcohol might be unable to stop themselves from drinking if there's a bottle of vodka in front of them, they can choose to avoid situations that might lead to drinking, and reach out for help and support.

Another reason many people feel powerless is that we often believe our actions don't make any difference. In this culture, we are often made to feel that we must do something big or grand to matter or generate any sort of effective change. This leads to a lot of people that do nothing because they feel their actions are insignificant. The reality is that our actions ripple out into the world in ways we could never imagine. What if Rosa Parks had never refused to give up her seat? The key is acting, not out of certainty that what we do will change the world, but out of passion and love. A mother does not pull her child out of the street because people are watching or she thinks it will put her on the news. When we love something more than ourselves, no action is too small.

Questions:

1. In what ways have you given away your power or blamed external people and circumstances for your problems?

2. What areas of your life do you have control over?

3. What would it be like to take responsibility for all of our mistakes and actions?

4. What are some actions that you haven't taken because they seemed small or insignificant?

5. What would it be like if you acted from love and passion rather than a desire to see a large outcome? How would it make you feel? How would it change the way you see yourself and the world?

CHAPTER 18
MY BEST FRIEND

MATTHEW

My best friend in the whole world is a fiery redhead named Jess. She is one of the most stubborn, reliable, frustrating and compassionate human beings I have ever met. We met at a party a few years ago. Jess was just out of college, and at a point in her life where she was trying to blow off some steam and have fun. I have an unfortunate habit of going up to every ginger I meet, saying, "Hi, Ginger!" Thankfully, my awkward attempts to be funny and make friends didn't creep her out too much. We had a really amazing conversation and I got her number. We ended up making plans to hang out.

It was a few minutes after the time we had planned to hang out, and I gave her a call. Jess told me she had completely forgotten we had made plans, but I said I was still up for spending time with her. She told me from the onset she was in a committed long distance relationship. We quickly started spending a lot of time together. She was very outdoorsy, intelligent and fun to be with. I introduced her to my friends, and we all became close. She had so many incredible aspirations, but a lot of the people she hung out with, and decisions she was making, kept her from pursuing them. She eventually stopped spending time with people who weren't supporting her dreams, and started using her freed-up energy to follow those dreams.

Another interesting side effect of having a female best friend is every time she starts dating someone, I have to convince her new partner that I don't have any intention of dating her. We have such a strong "friend zone" culture, and how guys are just waiting for their chance to score. I also find it very odd and lame that we often describe men's relationships with women like they were a sports game; first base, scoring, and things like that. Personally, this narrative has caused me to miss out on getting to know so many amazing people, and a lot of loneliness. Friendships are one of the most important parts of being happy and fulfilled in life. I am so grateful to have Jess as my friend. She is one of the largest pillars of support and stability in my life.

Lesson: Embracing unconditional love.

I have learned an amazing amount about trust and unconditional love from knowing Jess. I'm incredibly grateful I was able to move past the idea that the only value someone has to me is their physical appearance. I think ultimately we are all looking for unconditional love and acceptance, but we have a hard time accepting what it may look like, and being able to give it ourselves. One of the greatest lessons in my life has been to let go of my expectations and accept life and love as it is. It has led to more amazing and fulfilling connections with other people than I could have envisioned. Imagine what it would be like to live our lives from this space of unconditional love, regardless of our external circumstances or the issues facing us in our relationships and life situations.

Many people often equate love with codependent attachment, so to be clear; I don't mean codependent love with poor boundaries. However, what if it were possible to see through our fears, hurt, anger, pride, narcissism and all forms of emotional baggage to the core of love that resides in the heart of us and every person we meet? What if it were possible to live our lives from this space of unconditional love?

At the end of the day, this love is all that matters. Living from a space of this profound love and joy is possible, but most of us are too busy pursuing other goals we think will make us happy, to stop and become fully present in the moment and really see the remarkable and profound beauty within ourselves and others. Just know, another way of living is possible that is firmly rooted in unconditional love and is grounded in the wisdom of the ages. This love is practical, and doesn't mean we don't take care of the responsibilities in our lives. It just means we are willing to follow a higher call, and become more present to the deeper truth of love that is at the core of our being, and hides behind the mask that we wear.

Questions:

1. What does unconditional love mean to you?

2. What barriers do you have giving and accepting love and support?

3. How could you open yourself up more to love and connection in your life ?

CHAPTER 19
THE GIFT OF PAIN

"The Buddha called suffering a holy truth, because our suffering has the capacity of showing us the path to liberation. Embrace your suffering and let it reveal to you the way to peace."

– Thich Nhat Hanh

MATTHEW

My grandfather was an orthopedic surgeon. When my dad was in preschool, his family moved to Ethiopia so my grandfather could do medical mission work, helping local people including leprosy patients. Leprosy is a virus that targets the nervous system and kills the nerves, so someone stops feeling pain. While at first thought that sounds like a great thing, it is quite horrible for people suffering from it. Because they don't feel pain, they will often stick their hands in fires, or not notice cuts until they have become infected. Untreated infections kill the flesh around the area of infection, so it is quite common to see sufferers of leprosy missing limbs and covered in scabs.

My grandfather would take tendons from another part of the body and put them in the affected area, giving someone who had been crippled by leprosy range of motion so they could walk and use their limbs again. The villagers my grandfather worked with said he had magic in his fingers, and he was a great shaman. The body has a pain response for a reason, and when it is cut off there can be serious consequences.

STEVEN

When I was very young, we were driving across the country on a family trip and my mom remembers asking, "Where's Steve?" As Mom tells the story, this was fifty miles down the road after our family had stopped for lunch at a park in the middle of a random town. Apparently, they had left me at the park almost an hour before and no one had noticed. They went back, and there I was, sitting in the park, right where they had left me. I don't remember that incident, but I do remember a time when I was in elementary school. I was sneaking around our very large house, trying to see if I could get through every room without being seen. I could, and there was no one in my reality to know this but me.

This was a sad metaphor for my life at that time. Day after day, week after week, and year after year, I had the experience of isolation and feeling rejected. These core emotional wounds of feeling alone, unseen, inadequate and not important lingered on in the years since my childhood, and in some ways, still haunt me today. Facing and healing the emotional pain of isolation and loneliness leads me to the experience of more emotional connection with others.

Later in my early 20s, I was engaged to be married to my high school sweetheart. A few months before the wedding, we called it off because I was still Peter Pan and wasn't ready to grow up just yet. We loved each other deeply, but sometimes that's not enough. When the feelings of grief and loss finally hit me some months later, it was incredibly devastating and overwhelming. That loss was one of the most painful, powerful, and life-changing experiences of my life. This profound grief became a portal of transformation that led me to deeper and more fulfilling relationships. The intensity of my emotions over this loss cracked open my emotional walls, and ultimately helped me face my fears, release the pain of my emotional isolation, and emerge from the dysfunctional patterns of my past into a healthier adult life.

Lesson: Finding healing and connection by embracing our emotions and pain.

Pain is necessary feedback to protect us. In the same way, so are painful emotions. Fear, sadness, anger, guilt, grief and other negative emotions are actually powerful motivators and warning signs that tell us if we need to act or something is wrong. We have a culture that teaches us from a young age to suppress most of these emotions, especially for men. The result is we are emotional lepers, unaware of how unaddressed stress and emotional wounds damage us until something dramatic happens, like a depression episode or mental breakdown.

When an entire culture is doing this, there are incredible consequences. For instance, we ignore the impact our wars have on others or the damage we are doing to our environment. Someone who feels anger or guilt against the status quo is often shamed or told they are being dramatic. We will not grow until we face our fears. We can grow in a proactive manner, or we can wait until life smacks us down because we have avoided the problem until the resulting crisis hits us square between the eyes.

Most of us avoid our emotional pain and consequently continue to stay stuck in dysfunctional patterns of behavior. We recreate the cycles of conflict and suffering from our past until we are finally ready to learn from our experiences, growing out of the limitations of past conditioning. Many of us have to experience pain and loss of some kind before we are ready to release the ghosts of our past and mature into healthier choices and a better way of living. It's not necessary to go through these problems if we are willing to look in the mirror, be honest with ourselves, and go through our healing process in a more proactive manner.

Whether we are dealing with our losses and fears individually or collectively, our pain is simply another chance to heal and grow. I encourage us to take an honest look within ourselves and face the issues and fears that hold us back in our lives. This is a path to step into the greater joy of living a more real, honest and authentic life.

Today, I am greatly blessed to have an amazing depth of intimacy and mutual love with my wife, children, family and friends. Going through that grief helped me melt the walls of isolation and shame I had carried with me from my past. I am forever grateful for the experience of grief over this loss, and I wouldn't change a thing.

Facing pain and releasing our fears is the key to transformation. As a counselor, that experience gives me a powerful relationship with my clients in the counseling process when they are facing pain, regardless of the circumstances surrounding their emotional suffering. I wouldn't want to take away that emotional suffering, because they can experience transformation and healing through facing and embracing it. I know down to the marrow of my bones, the way to emotional freedom lies in facing, embracing, and going through the emotional suffering to get to the transformation on the other side.

Questions:

1. What are some ways you numb and suppress your feelings?

2. What causes you to get overwhelmed and numb your feelings?

3. What would it look like if you allowed yourself to feel more fully?

CHAPTER 20
A FATHER'S LOVE

STEVEN

It all started innocently enough. Matthew's younger brothers, strapped in their car seats, were falling asleep. Matthew, though nodding off, was still awake and sitting in his car seat. We were coming home on the freeway from Grandma's house, and I was feeling tired and cranky after a long day. At that moment, my highest priority was for all my little ones to go to sleep so Daddy could have some down time. I decided to pull the old "drive around a little more so everyone would go to sleep" trick. As soon as I passed the exit to our house, I heard Matthew exclaim from the back of the van, "Where you going? You're going the wrong way!"

Quickly, I tried to explain myself, but most of all I wanted to get Matthew quiet so he wouldn't wake up his brothers. No such luck. Matthew let his frustration be known in no uncertain terms, and the more I tried to quiet him, the louder and more upset he got. I tried placating him; no dice. I used the stern tone of voice; nope. Threats didn't work. This whole time, Matthew was repeating himself louder and louder saying, "You're going the wrong way! I want to go home now!"

Each time I tried to assure him I was going home as fast as possible, he simply got louder. After some time, I realized Matthew had gone over the edge, and I was feeling a little crazy myself. By this point, I had completely gone into survival mode, and had decided getting home was the top goal of the moment. Rather than stop the car and wring his neck, I just grimly maintained my silence and tried to get home as fast as possible.

Miraculously, the twins slept through the whole thing. As we neared our home, I stupidly told Matthew we were almost home, only to hear him say, "I don't want to go home!" Right then, I realized I was not dealing with a rational being. Judging from the intensity of my anger, and the fantasies of the dire retribution I was about to exact on my eldest three-year-old son, I realized I was only barely hanging on to any semblance of rational thought myself.

As I pulled into the driveway, I resolved to let my wife, Liz, deal with our eldest while I carried the twins to bed and got myself to a calm place.

Liz had seen our van pull up, and quickly assessed the situation as she came out to greet us. She took Matthew into the living room, and allowed him to vent his frustrations while I carried the twins upstairs to bed, one at a time. As I held Craig, he sleepily raised his head enough to ask, "Why is Matthew crying?" before his head fell back on my shoulder, fast asleep once more. After the twins were tucked in, I took a few deep breaths, and quietly regained my composure before joining Matthew and Liz on the couch in the living room.

My anger was beginning to settle, and Matthew was somewhat calmer as well, However, when I joined them on the couch, he repeatedly told Liz he wanted Daddy to go away. I maintained my silence, looking for an opportunity to enter the conversation.

Finally, after more expressions of his anger, Matthew said, "I want to burn Daddy's work clothes!"

This sparked my interest, and I quickly asked Matthew, "Do you want to burn my play clothes, too?"

"No!" my strong-willed eldest emphatically replied. Immediately he restated, "I want to burn your work clothes!"

Right then, it hit me like a ton of bricks. I sat there as the heat slowly spread up my neck and to my face. I remembered how I had been working an unusually excessive amount the past month. I'd been out of town at conferences for two weeks straight and had been putting in extra hours before and after the trip to make up for lost time at work. My family, and more specifically at this moment, my eldest son, had been feeling the pinch of my absence.

I had been fooling myself up to this point, believing I'd lined up so much support from family and friends during my absence. I had been thinking about how my kids would be fine with all of these wonderful people around them while I was away. I realized just then that Matthew had gotten precious little of his father's love and attention over the past month. When he did get my attention, I had given it only grudgingly, being more concerned with my own agenda. In that moment, I understood I was the fool, and no matter who else was involved, nothing could ever replace a father's love.

These ideas came to me in a brief flash of insight lasting less than a second. I checked out these thoughts with Matthew who quickly agreed that I was indeed on the right track. Matthew, feeling that I had finally gotten the message, climbed out of his mother's lap and came and sat in mine. I held him quietly for a long time as he leaned against my chest. I felt such conflicting emotions. I was acutely aware of deep love for my precious son, while at the same time feeling intense shame for being so wrapped up in my work that I had forgotten about what was most important in my life. As I sat there tightly holding my son, there was no doubt in my mind nothing could ever replace a father's love.

Valentine's Day note from Matthew seven years later

Dear Dad,

You're the best. You always listen to me and you're very understanding. You do a lot of activities with me like jogging. You answer all my questions and you know a lot of interesting subjects! Happy Valentine's Day.

Love,

Matt

Lesson: Love shown by consistent, positive attention is vital for a child's healthy development.

As parents, our time, energy, and positive attention are the greatest gifts we can give our children. We often get so busy with our lives, we forget to give ourselves to the people that matter most to us. Children who lack consistent, positive attention from their parents tend to have poorer self-images, more acting-out behaviors, reduced achievement, and increased family conflict.

As parents, we may not realize the larger-than-life position we hold in our children's psyche. Our consistent, positive attention assures them the world is a safe place and everything is okay. This gives our children a foundation from which they can learn, grow, and explore the world without unnecessary fear getting in the way. Our kids can actually show more intelligence and have more life-energy to bring to their daily concerns when they feel the emotional support of their parents. Conversely, the residual anxiety created in children by overly critical or inattentive parents takes up brain processing space in our children's developing brains and leaves them with less energy to deal with their daily lives.

Proactive parenting time spent now saves us time and energy because we have less conflict later.

Making parenting a priority can actually save us time and energy by minimizing the time spent in crisis management with our children and by reducing the stress of family conflict. A small amount of consistent and daily positive attention is so easy for us to give, costs so little, and has such powerful, lasting, and profound effects on our children.

Listen to children to understand the unexpressed and unmet needs influencing their misbehavior.

This experience with Matthew taught me to not always immediately react to my children's overt behavior, but rather to look for the unexpressed and unmet needs that are influencing their misbehavior. If I had blindly reacted to Matthew's tantrum with frustration, or by immediately giving him consequences, I never would have learned why he was acting out. If I had let my anger control my reactions to my son, then I would have created more mistrust and hurt between Matt and myself which would have subtly reinforced his feelings of hurt and anger leading to more acting-out behavior.

Instead, when I took the time to understand why Matthew was upset, everything changed and I actually formed a deeper bond of trust with my son, which continues today.

Children need limits. However, immediately giving consequences or setting limits may not always be the best response to our kids' misbehavior. Taking the time to understand their point of view allows them to feel heard and understood which increases trust and communication in the family.

Listening to our children's concerns models healthy communication for them, and can also give us important information to help make more informed decisions when administering discipline. In short: a little understanding goes a long way.

A father's love revisited.

When I was 15, I thought my father was a jerk who was continually on my back. He always had me working on something, whether it was my homework, cleaning the rain gutters, or mowing the lawn. I wanted him to talk, listen, and take more time with me. When we did connect, it was while working together, like when we built a stand for my keyboard in the garage with his power tools. My dad was always working. That was his thing, and as a teenager, I was always mad at him because I wanted him to be different.

One time he said to me, "Steve, out of all my children, I think you gave me the most trouble," and I believe that was probably true. It was not that I did a lot of bad stuff in middle school or high school. I was just in his face more than my siblings, and I repeatedly challenged him when I did not like something he did or did not do. A few years later, at a personal growth seminar, I realized that my dad had given me the best he had. He knew how to work, and that was what he taught me. I realized that his way of loving me was to teach me how to work. He was loving me in his own way, but I never understood that when I was a teenager.

I also realized that maybe he did not want to talk to me too much because I was always giving him a hard time, and our lack of communication was my responsibility. In that moment, I let go of my grudges toward my dad for not being what I wanted him to be, and I started loving him for the father he was. My dad was dependable and loyal to my mom and all of us children. He loved us, and was always even-tempered and fair in his judgments. He worked hard and provided whatever we needed, and he made sure all of his kids could pursue their dreams. While he hadn't been one to talk about his feelings or listen to my problems, he gave me the best he had every single day of his life.

When these thoughts hit me, I immediately called my dad and apologized for giving him such a hard time over the years. I admitted that I had been the jerk in our relationship. I told him I realized that his pushing me to work was his way of loving me, and I thanked him for giving me such a good work ethic, which has been such an asset in my life. I also asked him if we could start over and have a better relationship, and from that day on, my communication with him has been remarkable. After that, he always approached me with a hug and said, "I love you."

Let me say a little more about my dad. He was an orthopedic surgeon, and when I was little, he and my mom moved the family to Ethiopia where he was a medical missionary for quite some time. My father pioneered crucial techniques in surgery on leprosy patients, and after some years in the mission field, he came back to the United States and enrolled orthopedic surgeons from around the country to go over to Ethiopia. They stayed year-round in month-long shifts to teach the Ethiopian doctors about orthopedic surgery. Because of my dad, they now have orthopedics in Ethiopia. He is truly a great man, and today I am proud to be his son. However, I still remember that when I was 15, I thought he was a jerk who was always on my back.

Lesson: Happiness comes from changing our perspective.

Mark Twain once said that when he was 15, his dad didn't know anything, but when he turned 25, he was amazed at how much his father had learned in ten years. For me, I gained the relationship with my dad that I had always wanted when I let go of my resentment toward him, and began to love him for who he was. My father began to open up to me when I stopped blaming and criticizing him. Suddenly, he transformed before my eyes, but the person who changed was not him, but me. He had unconditionally and truly loved me all along. I just wasn't able to see it at the time.

Today, as I look at my own incredible sons, I finally understand how my dad felt about me, and I'm so thankful I had my father. I am grateful that his loving me all these years has helped me open my eyes and learn how to see.

Like in my relationship with my father, forgiveness is essentially seeing through the illusion of our fears and understanding the truth of the essential goodness of ourselves and those around us. It is about releasing judgments that cause resentment and block communication. The way to find happiness in life is to forgive ourselves and others. Forgiveness is not about overlooking others' faults or bad behavior. It's about realizing we misunderstood the other person in a fundamental way. When we want others to be something they are not, we set up ourselves for frustration and heartache. When others do not live up to our expectations, we hold resentment, which creates barriers and blocks to healthy communication.

Take a moment to look behind the mask. If we get closer to the person we judge and understand them better, we might be surprised. This is not about letting others off the hook for poor behavior. It's about seeking first to understand; taking accountability for our own character defects and poor choices, creating a positive emotional environment where we have a better chance to successfully address our differences with others.

All of us act out because of our emotional wounds. Look past surface appearances to see the good in another person, and we will see the good in ourselves. Help to understand and have compassion for the wounds in others, and we will heal our own wounds as well. When we see through the labels we put on others, and consciously walk toward and through the fires of our anger and fear, we will find another being that is good on the inside, just like us. No one else needs to change for us to be happy. Our happiness or lack of it is our choice.

To some extent, we all live under the false assumption that we can only be happy when others in our lives change in some way. We hold grudges, complain, manipulate them to change, threaten, and finally, leave when we realize others are not going to change to suit us. This state of affairs gives us a sad life. Ultimately, our happiness is up to us and no one else.

Happiness comes through changing your perspective. Finding happiness only requires we change the way we look at others. As Wayne Dyer said, "Change the way you look at things, and the things you look at change." When we see our family, friends, and ourselves in a different light, they miraculously change right before our eyes into the people we have always wanted to have in our life.

Questions

1. What perspectives or beliefs do you have about life or people that keep you from being happy?

2. What would it be like to let go of these beliefs?

3. What are some beliefs you would like to change? What are a few steps you could take? This could look like writing a letter of forgiveness or having a conversation.

CHAPTER 21
HEALING YOUR FAMILY TREE

STEVEN

When my grandmother died in the hospital, she had lost all her teeth and her hair was gone due to chemotherapy. She had a good sense of humor, and made jokes about looking like an orangutan. The doctor had told her long before that either her lungs or her liver would get her, and in the end, the cancer had spread from her lungs all over her body. On the day she died, I remember walking away from the hospital after visiting her one final time, and thinking to myself, "Grandma, your body is broken, but your spirit is about to fly free!" She was an alcoholic who at one point would hide the bottles around the house, and through her life she had been a chain smoker. My grandfather had some issues with anger and enabling, and made a lot of money in lumber. This was on my mother's side, and my mom carried the emotional baggage from issues with her parents.

On my father's side, they were stoic, guarded, and emotionally shut down. My dad's ancestor was one of the last confederate soldiers to walk out of the battle of Atlanta when General Sherman burned it to the ground. My father told the story of how the men folk said he came back a war hero, and the women said he came back a broken man. This was true post-traumatic stress disorder, but they had no idea of any mental health treatment at that time. This emotional brokenness was passed down from father to son ever since then and possibly before.

The men in my father's family were from Pensacola, Florida, and they worked hard. They made good choices with money, and externally did well, but internally they were controlling and rigid, and emotional intimacy was not an option. My father told stories of how his parents sent him off to camp, all summer, every summer, and sent him to boarding school in high school so they wouldn't have to deal with him as a teenager.

My parents were great people in their own ways. They had good intentions and loved their family and friends the best they knew how, but both had their own emotional wounds. As I reflect on how these issues have impacted my life, I can clearly see how shame, anger, addiction and isolation in my family tree have affected me and my siblings. I've had to work on these emotional issues my entire life. Looking back, I can also see how this family legacy of trauma has impacted my character defects, and has consequently affected my sons through me.

I am deeply grateful for the healing process, and continue working to free my consciousness from the legacy of emotional suffering on both sides of my family. I embrace the gifts in this legacy as I continue to step into the wholeness of my essential self to the best of my ability.

Lesson: Understanding the big picture of our family patterns frees us from repeating them.

Our emotional issues are embedded in the history of our family trees as well. When we transform the problems and emotional breakdowns in our lives, we are healing our family tree and breaking the cycles of suffering passed down through our family lineage. It can be helpful to step back and look at the big picture of our path of growth in life, learning to understand and embrace the legacy of emotional suffering, and finding the joy in our family tree.

If we want to heal the family legacy of suffering and dysfunctional character traits passed on to us, it can be helpful to self reflect on the issues of dysfunction in our life, and how this relates to the emotional baggage we've learned. We are conditioned in the patterns of family dysfunction from not only our parents, but from our grandparents, and in the stories of our family tree. The apple doesn't fall far from the tree.

We are still responsible for our issues. Our parents, grandparents, and ancestors are not to blame because we have made the choices to perpetuate whatever problems and character defects we've learned from them. However, part of the healing process is doing our best to understand our personal issues and the legacy of dysfunction and emotional suffering in our family tree, so we can address these problems and transform our character defects and our family legacy.

As a counselor, I work with many individuals and families in the healing process, and we often consider these family patterns. Here are a few steps in healing our family tree that might be helpful in thinking about the healing process.

1. **Improve your self-awareness.** Understand your family patterns of conflict and the shared history of trauma that all members in your family have due to this common history. Everyone is impacted and each person may react to this shared history of trauma differently.

2. **Stop the blame game.** Be careful of the blame game and scapegoating. The blame game is the problem because however we define who the victim is, and who the perpetrator is in our personal and family story, these roles often switch. In family conflict, everyone is blaming each other on some level, thereby contributing to the problem. At one moment, a person could be the perpetrator, and later become the victim or rescuer, so these roles constantly shift.

3. **Own responsibility for your life.** To escape this cycle, we must own responsibility for how we blame our problems on others, and our role in the family pattern of conflict. Blaming ourselves is not accountability; it is just part of the shame that perpetuates the family dysfunction. Taking accountability is owning our character defects, and making positive change while appreciating the basic goodness of our humanity.

Questions:

1. What are some common dynamics or patterns of conflict in your family?

2. What can you take accountability for in those conflicts?

3. What are some new ways you could go about handling those conflicts and communicating with your family?

CHAPTER 22
MY MOTHER'S LOVE

"We are born out of love. Love is our mother."

- Rumi

STEVEN

My mother had requested for us to "sing her over" when she transitioned from this life to the next. When she died some years ago from complications of lung cancer, a few of my brothers, my father, my wife and I were around her bed singing, "Amazing Grace" when she took her final breath. We all hugged and cried, and these were the first tears I had ever seen from some of my brothers. We were together in a peaceful, silent, and loving space in the moments following Mom's transition. The connection I felt at that time with family and my mother was tender and genuine.

Mother's gift was to drive to the heart of a problem or challenge in any given situation. She had a talent for correctly identifying issues in people or situations with a certain intuitive accuracy that was often scary to those around her. In addition, she often lacked empathy. She could be harsh and insensitive to others' feelings when she was angry or caught in her zeal to get to the truth. This quality didn't always endear her to others, and when she passed, she had unresolved issues with many people.

Growing up, I frequently saw an angry, scary mom. I had trouble seeing through her intense emotions to the core truth of love and real connection that was always her deepest intention. As an adult, I have had to struggle with this anger within myself, and I've seen this family legacy of anger reflected in Matthew's struggles in his life challenges as well. Through my adult years, as I began to recognize and release my own fears and issues with my mother, I learned to see through emotional dysfunction to the core truth of love in my mother. Consequently, I was able to be less reactive to her anger, and develop a much closer and compassionate connection with her as I grew older.

At this point in my life, I get how deeply my mom loved me and all her children. After many years, I see that profound devotion in my relationship with her that I wasn't able to see before. Even though she didn't always express her love in the ways I wanted her to, I can feel the caring connection with Mom shining from the other side of the veil of life and death, and I am grateful for her love.

In the year before she died, I was with Mom in the emergency room when she got the news her lung cancer had returned. In that moment, she knew her days were limited on this earth, and she looked at me with fear in her eyes and said, "Steve, I know that you and I are straight and I don't need to say this to you, but I do take accountability for how I have screwed up many relationships in my life. I'm sorry for my actions and my part in creating the problems in our relationship in the past." Typically, my mom didn't apologize for anything, and this was only the third time I remembered her apologizing during her life.

Lesson: Holding our center in the midst of conflict.

Over the years, I learned how to stay in a relationship with my mother without becoming a doormat and without fighting. To do this in difficult relationships, we must be honest about our own issues without taking the other person's emotions personally. It takes avoiding both fight and flight, and finding the third option by simply holding our center, realizing another person's emotions are not our fault. We are not to blame for their anger or sadness. It is allowing the other person to have their emotions and letting ourselves have our own. When I could do this in my relationship with Mom, we always got along just fine. I was no longer dominated by the changes in her volatile emotions. Holding my center, no matter what emotions of praise or criticism anyone projects toward me, is what I do in my best moments with loved ones and in counseling. It creates a profound space of unconditional love that is beautiful and deeply satisfying.

When we are caught in the fears of our ego, everything we perceive will be a reflection of that fear. If we free our minds from these same ego fears, we begin to see the reflection of unconditional love that is at the heart of every human being. When we learn to look past our own ego fears, seeing through the illusion of the ego mask others around us are wearing, we begin to see heaven in relationships with our family, friends and associates.

Heaven is not a place or a time. It is a state of mind where we see through the illusion of our ego fears to understand and perceive the essential connection and oneness of all life as a unified whole. This is not some pie in the sky or useless philosophy. This kind of thinking is eminently practical, and empowers us to have relationships that work in our lives.

To practice this way of life, we start by shifting our beliefs, fears, and perceptual thought system rather than focusing on trying to fix or change other people or situations. Instead of going into fight or flight, we learn to hold our center and move synergistically with the people and events around us, finding a whole new level of power, clarity, and effectiveness in our lives.

Questions:

1. In what ways do you try to change other people in your life or make your happiness conditional on their actions?

2. What would life be like if you regarded everyone with unconditional acceptance and compassion?

3. What are some actions you can take to change how you relate to others in a more positive way?

CHAPTER 23

WE ARE ALL JUST ANGRY KITTENS

MATTHEW

During my first year working in drug and alcohol treatment, I had one of my most difficult clients. Thankfully, it was more mentally and emotionally challenging than any physical threat. Charlie was in his 40s and addicted to methamphetamine. He was constantly pushing boundaries, and would get incredibly angry and manipulative if what he wanted was challenged. From my perspective, most of the other counselors and therapists let him get his way. I was one of the only people that actually held him accountable. At the time, that was my interpretation of the situation. I was being a martyr, and believed I was the only one committed to holding the sacred boundaries of the program. It drove me crazy when Charlie didn't listen to me! He would constantly try to manipulate me, attempting to get other clients and counselors to back his story that I was a self-righteous asshole (which might have been true to some extent).

It got to the point where Charlie recorded everything that might have been construed as me breaking the rules. Some of his points were valid, and some not so much. He filed a grievance against me with the HR department while he was still in treatment, and I had to sit down with my manager and sign a performance plan. I was livid, and planned my counter attack. This client had been on a behavioral contract that he had violated several times. The contract essentially enforced the treatment boundaries. If you didn't uphold these expectations, you were out of the program. I felt that no one wanted to confront Charlie and hold him accountable, so I would! I went to his therapist since behavioral contracts were ultimately handled by therapists, and presented my case. "I can't believe Charlie isn't out of here by now! He is making this a hostile environment for the other clients and everyone who works here. He needs to go."

His therapist looked at me calmly. "Matt, you seem to feel personally attacked by Charlie. What is it about him that triggers you so much?"

I got very indignant. "It's not about me; it's about the program and the other clients. He is lowering our standard of care and impacting the experience of the participants because we have to spend so much time dealing with his bullshit."

His therapist responded, "Matt, if I felt Charlie was being detrimental to the experience of the other clients, I would get him out of this program today. If I kicked him out, he would be extremely high risk, and I need to balance that. Is he annoying? Yes, but in my mind, he hasn't done anything that would justify throwing him out onto the street. What is it about him that makes you so angry?"

I responded, "He doesn't listen to anything I or anyone else has to say. I mean we have rules for a reason."

Charlie's therapist responded, "Awe, so he doesn't listen to you. What a crime!"

"That's not what I meant," I quickly replied.

Without sounding unkind, Charlie's therapist gently said, "Matt, let's pretend you are taking care of a bunch of baby kittens, and one of them goes off and does his own thing. You pick up the kitten to take him back and he bites you. Would you be mad at the kitten? No! He's a fucking kitten!" Charlie's therapist continued, "In a similar way, Charlie, and a lot of the guys who come through this program, are hurting from years of neglect and heartache, and are emotionally stunted. Actually, we all are in a lot of ways. So, it doesn't make sense to get angry at someone for doing something that, in their world, is necessary for their self-preservation."

In that moment, I realized I was letting my own defensiveness and ego impact the way I was interacting with Charlie. While we absolutely need to hold boundaries and make sure the actions of others don't hurt us or other people, if we are acting from a triggered ego or anger, we will always cause more harm than good.

STEVEN

Many years ago, I was working in a juvenile justice detention center as a counselor.

Teens were incarcerated for longer periods of time, averaging six months to two years, due to the severity of the crimes they had committed. One of my clients was locked in an isolation cell at this detention facility for an extended period of time because he had brutally assaulted and injured another youth. We had a session for about an hour, and he proudly described his gang affiliation. He discussed how his brothers, cousins, uncles, and close friends who were in the gang together, protected his neighborhood from others who threatened his family and friends. He said he was willing to give his life to protect his community. As we talked, it became apparent how powerful and profound his love was for his family, friends and neighbors. Of course, he had a great deal of anger, rage, and trauma in his life, but I quickly realized what motivated this person in front of me was love, pure and simple.

Lesson: There is no "them" or "other." We are all on the same team.

Over and over again in my counseling practice, I see people who are deeply and passionately committed to their values, principles, and the people in their life. No matter what problems someone has, underneath their issues are individuals who profoundly love their family and friends. I always find this love at the core of the human experience, and. I can't help but feel the unconditional love that unites us in our common humanity.

We are taught from a very young age to constantly evaluate and judge others, and they are doing the same to us. If someone doesn't meet up to our expectations, we "other" them; putting them in the category of "less than," "not worth our time," or the "enemy." Othering and devaluing people is how wars and atrocities have been justified for thousands of years. While it is important to have boundaries and protect ourselves and our family, we can do so while still seeing the underlying humanity of the other person. The Dali Lama once famously said, if he faced an intruder, he would shoot him in the legs, then go over and stroke his head and take care of him. Even if someone opposes us, we can still treat them with love and compassion. Everyone has a different worldview and reasons for acting. If we don't agree with them, or need to hold them accountable, we can still do so with compassion.

> "If we could read the secret history of our enemies, we should find in each man's life sorrow and suffering enough to disarm all hostility."
>
> - Henry Longfellow

When we get closer to the person we judge, to understand them better, we might be surprised. This is not about letting others off the hook for poor behavior. It's about seeking first to understand, taking accountability for our own character defects and poor choices, to create a positive emotional environment where we have a better chance of successfully addressing our differences with others. All of us act out because of our emotional wounds. Look past surface appearances to see the good in another person, and we will see the good in ourselves. Our unconscious mind doesn't actually know the difference between blaming others and blaming ourselves. Regardless of whether we condemn others or ourselves, the negative emotions are residing in our psyche, impacting our mood and self-image.

When we criticize others, we criticize ourselves. When we harm others, we harm ourselves. When we judge others, we judge ourselves. Try to understand and have compassion for the wound in others, and we will heal our own wounds as well. Go with kindness toward the relationship or situation where we are the most hurt, the angriest, or the most afraid, because the wound is where the light enters us. When we see through the labels we put on others, and consciously walk toward and through the fires of anger and fear, we will find another being that is good on the inside, just like us. If we practice this on a daily basis, we'll begin to allow ourselves to have extraordinary experiences that have the power to lift us out of the ordinary ego-driven awareness where many of us frequently get stuck. This practice can lead to resolving any difficult pattern of conflicts or difficulties in our life, helping to create a life we love.

Questions:

1. Who do you see as the "other"? (Could be specific individuals, groups, organizations, political opinions, etc.).

2. How does seeing someone as the "other" impact the way you treat them?

3. What would it be like if you treated people you dislike with compassion and respect? Is it possible to hold boundaries and hold others accountable, and still have basic compassion and respect for them?

CHAPTER 24
LOVE IS NOT WEAK

MATTHEW

My dad and I recently ran our first seminar together. It was based around personal transformation and overcoming core fears to realize our authentic selves. The participants were mostly my father's clients, so he personally knew a lot about where they were struggling in their lives. One of the most impactful parts of the seminar happened around a man named Sam.

Sam's son was struggling with suicidal thoughts and behavior. When opening up about this situation, Sam expressed that he felt his son was overly sensitive and needed to control his emotions more. Sam felt his own emotions were dangerous and overwhelming, and he had learned to "turn them off." Upon repeating this to my dad, who can be very confrontational, he looked Sam dead in the eye and said, "That's bullshit. The problem is that you are afraid of your feelings."

I took a different tact and told Sam it was okay to feel his emotions were too overwhelming. While it was important to feel and express himself, it was all right if he needed to shut down and do it on his own terms. My dad and I had a small disagreement about how this was handled during our break. Coming back to the room, he addressed it head on and asked if Sam, or anyone else in the room, felt that he had gone over the top. Most everyone said they were grateful for my father calling out Sam, and thought he had been attacking the view that "numbing emotions was okay," and not Sam himself.

One woman said to Sam, "You are not bullshit, but that belief is bullshit and it is dangerous." Many other women expressed how the men in their lives shut down emotionally, and the harm it had caused them and those around them. My dad then shared that "love is not weak," and sometimes love means being direct and forceful.

My father asked Sam if he was all right to try something. He had Sam lay down in the middle of the room, and everyone put a hand under him. We all gave him affirmations and blessings. Sam admitted that he felt he was failing his son. My dad asked what it felt like to fail his son. Sam said, "I have words for a lot of things, but losing my son, I have no words for that. That is just pain."

We lifted up Sam as a collective, then put him down. Sam burst into tears at being held and supported by the group. My father addressed Sam after we got back into a circle and said, "Now, if you can do this with your son, authentically share the way you feel and how much you love him, that will open up a door for change."

Lesson: Learning to see love as a strength.

In our culture, we often see love as a weakness. Whether it's an evil villain in a movie exploiting a hero's relationship to someone they love, someone making irrational decisions out of love, or an individual taken advantage of by someone they love. I think this comes down to a misunderstanding of what love is. Love is not giving someone everything they want, or neglecting our own boundaries. Love might mean holding someone accountable. It could mean standing up for what we believe in. Nelson Mandela, Martin Luther King, and the Dali Lama, some of the strongest people in history, were motivated by love. Love means that we are willing to expand our sense of self to include someone else or something else. It can give us unimaginable strength and courage, allowing us to do things we never thought were possible.

Questions:

1. What does love mean to you?

2. What would it mean if you saw love as a strength and not a weakness? If you already see it as a strength, how has it helped you in life?

3. What would a life, basing your actions and decisions on love, look like?

CONCLUSION

MATTHEW

What do we love?

Undeniably, we are living in a time of unprecedented change. Our communities and environment are stretched to the breaking point, and the world is calling us to action. In the midst of this, a much more important question to ask than, "What are we afraid of?" is "What do we love?" Action is much more powerful from love than from fear. I love this amazing planet. I cherish the mountains, the ocean, the trees, and the amazing diversity of life. I adore my family, my friends, and the people around me. All of the silly and crazy things humans do from love, including our incredible works of art, compassion and beauty. When we frame the problem in terms of survival, we naturally shut down from the conversation. Something vastly more important than our survival is at stake. This grand world of beauty and life. I am grateful to have so many inspiring, beautiful, and powerful people around me that are already willing to live the change they want to see in the world. So, I ask you, "What do you love? What do you have to protect? And what kind of a world do you want to create?"

STEVEN

As I read Matthew's words in the previous section, I am struck by the remarkable transformation from fear to love he has experienced and is now living out in the world. At a recent yoga and meditation class led by Matthew, many people came up to me after and let me know what a remarkable person he is. Through the emotional pain and depths of his struggles, Matthew has found a deep and abiding love. He has learned to channel his intense warrior energy from anger and hurt, to love. He stands for his authentic love in a powerful and unapologetic manner. Through these experiences, Matthew has developed a depth of character I truly admire.

My journey with Matthew has been one of the most difficult and powerfully transformative turning points in my life. There were times when I had no idea how we would get through some of the moments, but the growth that has come out of these experiences is profound, and has transformed me as much as it has my son.

I think about all the parents in the world who are raising emotionally intense children, and I am reminded of a quote from Rumi that states, "The cure for pain is in the pain." In facing the anguish and grief, Matthew and I have found a deeper appreciation of others, ourselves, and of life itself. I am grateful for all of it. I also offer encouragement to all parents who struggle with the often painful and difficult moments of parenting their children and teens. I celebrate the joy and profound connection with our children that shines through all of these experiences.

www.ingramcontent.com/pod-product-compliance
Ingram Content Group UK Ltd.
Pitfield, Milton Keynes, MK11 3LW, UK
UKHW022237230426
12048UKWH00018BA/1311